DOVE SONG

PECULIAR WORKS

The Fob Bible
Out of the Mount
Fire in the Pasture
Monsters & Mormons
Dorian
States of Deseret
Seasons of Change
Dove Song

DOVE SONG

Heavenly Mother
IN MORMON POETRY

EDITED BY

Tyler Chadwick

Dayna Patterson

Martin Pulido

ⵎ
PECULIAR PAGES

Dove Song: Heavenly Mother in Mormon Poetry
edited by Tyler Chadwick, Dayna Patterson, & Martin Pulido

Anthology copyright 2018 Peculiar Pages
Contributions copyright 2018 Individual contributors

ISBN: 978-1-7320302-1-3 (paperback, Ingram)
ISBN: 978-1-7320302-0-6 (paperback, CreateSpace)
ISBN: 978-1-7320302-2-0 (ebook, all formats)

Editors: Tyler Chadwick, Dayna Patterson, & Martin Pulido
Cover art: *Compression* by Denise Gasser
Cover design: Chrissy Ellsworth and Lynsey Jepson
Book design and digitization: Elizabeth Beeton

Published By:
PECULIAR PAGES
115 Ramona Avenue
El Cerrito, CA 94530
PeculiarPages.com

in collaboration with

B10 Mediaworx
PO Box 1233
Liberty, MO 64069-1233
b10mediaworx.com

CONTENTS

PART ONE

A Mother There
[1844 – 1910]

PART TWO

On the Far Shore
[1973 – 2003]

ILLUSTRATIONS

Proselytizing by a Marian Shrine in Québec

Women walk *chemin du rosaire* in morning's
cold white dresses. Wrapped in our cloaks we weather
snowy shoulders, withering stares. Take a card, *ma
dame?* In her eyes, were

years that gathered, ran down the well-worn grooves of
tears. *Est-ce que vous priez à elle?* We answer,
Non. She shakes the grief from her voice and welcomes
us to a service.

How can I, a traveler here, a woman
ask these devotees to abandon Mary?
In my mind, a feminine goddess, throneless,
wanders. We enter.

Je vous salue, Marie pleine... echoes through the
dim-lit nave. The arches, her fingers, bend and
hold. The windows pierce in between and make a
diadem. *Mère de*

Dieu, a wonder, hunger for softer gods is
spreading. Thousands blink at the endless prayers
spilled on lonely Father gods. Heaven's Mother,
where have we hidden?

Plant our souls with psalms for the Queen of Heaven.
Teach us dove song; lead us to lust for peacetime.
Wizen mouths. Enlarge our small hearts. Forgive us,
gentle us, Mother.

—*Dayna Patterson, 2010*

FOREWORD

TYLER CHADWICK

DAYNA PATTERSON

MARTIN PULIDO

The Hebrew Bible's Exodus narrative opens with the children of Israel in bondage to the Egyptians. Enter Moses, a Hebrew by birth who was allowed to live because the Hebrew midwives ignored Pharaoh's decree that all newborn Israelite boys should be killed. Hidden away for several months, he's eventually sent downriver where he's adopted by Pharaoh's daughter and grows up in Pharaoh's household. As a young adult, he observes the Hebrews' oppression and, standing up for a Hebrew man, kills an Egyptian. Fleeing into exile to avoid Pharaoh's anger, he marries and begins a new life in the wilderness as shepherd of his father-in-law's flocks.

The story of his divine call to return to Egypt as prophet and deliverer of Israel is widely-known and repeated. Drawn to Horeb, "the mountain of God," he hears God speaking "in a flame of fire from within a bush." Turning from the work of tending his father-in-law's flock, he approaches the bush to see how it burns without being consumed and God tells him to remove his sandals because the place is "holy ground" (NET [New English Translation], Exodus 3:1–5). In Cecil B. DeMille's Biblical epic, *The Ten Commandments* (1956), God's words (voiced by the late Donald Hayne) rumble from the bush, sending Charlton Heston-as-Moses to his knees. Prostrate before the deep-voiced God of his father, Moses commits to carry God's name from the encounter, to hold it up before Israel, and to lead Israel out of Egypt, to freedom.

As we consider this story now, after working for years on this anthology and exploring for longer the Divine Feminine in Mormonism, two questions come to mind: first, why must God be a dramatic *basso profondo*? And second, what might it look like to approach—and attempt to grasp and sustain—the holy?

In response to the first question, we hear the poets whose work we've gathered in *Dove Song* bearing witness that He doesn't. In fact, Mormonism says, God isn't simply a He, God's also a She—God's a They, a union of Eternal Beings. But what, pray tell, might They sound like? And more apropos to the anthology's concerns, what in particular might God the Mother's voice add to the chorus? Joseph Smith described "the voice of Jehovah," whom Latter-day Saints take to be the Son and recognize as acting and speaking after the manner of the Father, "as the sound of the rushing of great waters" (Doctrine & Covenants 110:3). While this may capture one aspect of the Father's verbal register, it may also echo how the Mother sounds. If not, we may only ever be able to guess what Mother sounds like, especially when the largely patriarchal voice of Mormon discourse (as of Western discourse in general) dominates religious conversations. Nevertheless, as compilers and editors of this collection, we've tried to showcase poems that imagine the potential range and register of Mother's voice as performed by many poets from the lush field of LDS Mormonism.

To organize this abundance, we've arranged the anthology in

a loosely chronological order, while at the same time attempting to keep each poet's poems together. This hasn't always been possible, since the writing lives of some poets span multiple decades and since the three-part structure we've chosen for the book splits the contemporary era into two discrete sections. (The work of five poets, Janice Allred, Joanna Brooks, Alex Caldiero, Maxine Hanks, and Melody Newey Johnson, appears in both sections.) At first blush, this separation might appear unnecessary; but as we kept company with the poems from the 1970s to today, we noticed a definite tonal shift in the early 2000s. Whereas the poems featured in Part One—many of them written by early Church leaders—speak with authority about and adoration of "the Eternal Mother,"[1] "Queen of Heaven,"[2] the poems in Part Two in general express grief, sorrow, and bitterness that Mother is largely absent from Mormon culture and discourse, an absence illustrated in *Dove Song* with the lack of poems from the 1920s through the 1960s.

This noticeable void in the anthology may mark a reduction in references to Heavenly Mother in the Mormon poetry published during those decades; while our research uncovered some poems addressing Heavenly Mother during this period (including works by C. E. Richardson, Anna Johnson, Margaret Tuttle Goff Sanchez, and Walter M. Horne), we didn't feel that the aesthetic or theological characteristics of those poems were pronounced enough to merit their inclusion among other texts that do rich aesthetic and/or theological work. *Dove Song*

---

1 See the excerpt from Eliza R. Snow's "To Mrs. [Sylvia Sessions] Lyon" (Trail Diary Version), p. 37.

2 See W. W. Phelps' "A Song of Zion," p. 31.

is a selective anthology, and that may create improper expect-
ations for readers who view it as an exhaustive historical
chronicle. In addition, researching this period has been more
difficult with sparser digital records, meaning that there may be
more to uncover in that period, including non-English works
published outside the United States.

Regardless, notable Mormon writers no longer included
Heavenly Mother as a topic of literary reflection in that period.
The resurgence and tonal shift in the 1970s grew out of a
response by LDS women to their dwindling participation in
religious practices during those prior decades. LDS women had
been censored from giving blessings and from offering opening
and closing sacrament meeting prayers and the rather
autonomously run Relief Society was realigned by church
correlation into a "priesthood auxiliary" to make it more
"priesthood-centered." This had incredible impact on the
society's focus, teachings, publications, financing, and social
services operations. LDS women were upset and found in
poetry an outlet for that frustration. Linda Sillitoe observed of
this time period: "Anger has become an acceptable emotion for
women to experience, let alone display, only recently—if at
all. [...] In most of the angry poems I have seen, the anger is
directed toward personal or institutional absences; the anger
represents the rejection of rejection."[3] For the first time, LDS
women were vocalizing in art their complicated experience
within the cultural and theological mores of their church.

They brought up Heavenly Mother to support their

---

3 "New Voices, New Songs: Contemporary Poems by Mormon Women," *Dialogue: A Journal of Mormon Thought*, vol. 13, no. 4, 1980, p. 57.

arguments and frustration. For instance, in the heat of the Equal Rights Amendment (ERA) debate, feminist activist Sonia Johnson had an airplane fly overhead trailing a banner noting that Heavenly Mother supported the ERA. It's no surprise that Heavenly Mother appeared in LDS women's poetry that grappled with women's religious marginalization. They saw the Mother as a symbol for that marginalization, both in suffering it Herself and as an audience to hear their plight and even reveal a remedy. The poetry in Part Two of *Dove Song* tackles both these challenges of gender inequality by either directly confronting them (see Munk and Wallace, for instance) or by reenvisioning Heavenly Mother as more proactive and involved in the roles typically associated with Heavenly Father (see Pearson and Sillitoe). The latter texts became a means of correcting in heaven what was unequal on earth with its patriarchal ecclesiastical structure and social norms. This shift in content is paralleled by tremendous shifts in form and tone, as if the old literary conventions themselves were something to be overcome.

Hence, the section division for Part Three, which signals the aforementioned tonal shift. While the poems in Part Three— *Dove Song*'s largest section, although it represents only a decade's worth of writing—don't deny the abiding grief, sorrow, bitterness, frustration, or anger many Mormons feel over Mother's long discursive absence, they also take Her as a given and revel in the space poetry provides to explore new possibilities for understanding, honoring, celebrating, and connecting with Her. More, they echo trends in contemporary LDS art that envision women no longer as merely the faithful saved (recipients of light, revelation, and salvation), at the periphery of the scene, sitting in awe and adoration at the knees of male prophets, male angels, and the Son of God. They are cast in salvific roles themselves—as bearers of lights, as leaders, as angelic beings offering comfort, support, and announcing the love of God. In the visual arts, this can be seen prominently in the works of Annie Henrie Nader, Brian Kershisnik, J. Kirk Richards, and Caitlin Connolly (the latter two have portrayed Heavenly Mother repeatedly).

We can't be fully certain, but we suspect that this assumption of Heavenly Mother as a granted aspect of Mormon doctrine may emerge from contemporary Western culture's focus on and gradual acceptance of the equal rights of men and women, as well as from increased reference to Heavenly Parents in official Church discourse.[4] And broader acceptance of Heavenly Mother as a "cherished and distinctive"[5] doctrine seems to have made speaking and writing about Her a much less fraught activity than it once was. When combined with the expansive state of contemporary Mormon poetry, the growing institutional recognition that Mother stands beside Father at the center of LDS theology seems to have stirred the emergence of an abundant field of poetry that contemplates Mother and Her role in our lives. The texts in this field include pieces published for the A Mother Here: Art and Poetry Contest, which Martin Pulido and Caroline Kline hosted in 2014, as well as poems

---

4 See Christian Anderson, "Heavenly Parents at General Conference," *Zelophedad's Daughters*, 1 November 2016, zelophehadsdaughters.com/2016/11/01/heavenly-parents-at-conference/. Accessed 5 February 2018.

5 "Mother in Heaven," *LDS.org*, October 2015, lds.org/topics/mother-in-heaven. Accessed 5 February 2018.

gathered through the open call for poetry we distributed in 2015.

Which brings us back to our earlier question: what might it look like to approach—and attempt to grasp and sustain—the holy? Per Moses' story, the approach looks like turning from everyday concerns to consider how common objects, like a hillside bush, might flicker with God's presence and glory; and also per Moses, the attempt to grasp and sustain the holy looks like holding in mind and holding out to others the objects, language, and metaphors through which we meet God and give shape and/or meaning to our experience of God. Gathering the poems for this project and considering together the vital presence of God the Mother in Mormon poetry and theology, we've felt like Moses approaching that hillside bush and attempting to comprehend and bear witness of the holiness he found there. This isn't by any means to say that we fancy ourselves prophets and deliverers chosen of God to save God's people. No, by that we simply mean that as scholars and poets who are invested in Mormonism, we've felt drawn to turn our attention to the presence of Mother smoldering in the brush of Mormon thought. Smoldering, though, isn't the right word for what we found. Rather, exploring the expansive field of Mormon poetry that contemplates Heavenly Mother, we've seen not smoldering ashes in the underbrush but a many-colored flame building within and whispering from a sacred Mother Tree.

And here we've shifted the burning bush metaphor in light of *Dove Song*'s interest in the Divine Feminine, bringing the narrative of Moses' encounter with God into conversation with a more directly Mormon text: Book of Mormon prophet Jacob's telling of the allegory of the olive tree. In this narrative, a man worries over his vineyard, fertilizing his olive trees, aerating the soil around their roots, and pruning their branches to preserve the health of each tree and its fruit, to keep them from growing wild. While tending to his favored tree, he sees signs of distress and decay in the plant and turns his full attention to nurturing it back to vitality. He dungs it. He digs about the roots. He prunes it, and with his servant's help, grafts some branches into other trees while planting other branches elsewhere in the vineyard and grafting branches from other trees into his favored tree—all to cultivate and preserve his favored tree's health, productivity, and biological heritage. The scriptural account likens this tree unto the house of Israel and can be interpreted as arguing for God's abiding attentiveness to Israel's seed such that it might propagate to fill and bless the earth. However, the story's clear concern for the vigor of what it finally and repeatedly calls the vineyard's "mother tree" (Jacob 5:54, 56, 60) opens possibilities for reading the figure as a benevolent feminine influence whose presence brings glory, strength, goodness, and joy to the vineyard and its vast ecology just as she receives these things in return (5:54, 59, 60).

Like the allegorized vineyard workers laboring to preserve their mother tree, we've sensed a compelling need to focus attention on the work of cherishing God the Mother and acknowledging Her influence among Her children by presenting and celebrating Her abiding and expansive presence in the literary and theological handiwork of a diverse group of Mormon writers. While, as the visual and verbal imagery bound up in the phrase "dove song" suggests, this work has emerged from a sense of mourning and loss, it also reaches to share the peace, power, and grace that emanate from our Mother Tree: "the throne of the Great Eternal Mother" (to borrow from Eliza R. Snow).[6]

It has been humbling—and a deep honor—to attend to this work together as we've compiled *Dove Song* and, through the process, to feel that we've been handling the holy. We've had the pleasure of getting to the heart of Mormon theology, which as Dallin H. Oaks has put it, "begins with heavenly parents."[7] Heavenly Mother is the capstone to Joseph Smith's explosive and radical theological output during the Church's Nauvoo period. The revelation of Heavenly Mother wasn't adding an additional deity to some Mormon pantheon of gods, akin to adding a Hera to a Zeus; rather, it redefined the very nature of what it meant to be God. Through his unveiling of Heavenly Mother, Joseph can be seen asserting that the world possesses radical alterity—that its products and inhabitants possess differences that are, at root, real and irreducible. In the theology emerging from Joseph's teachings, God is a Many (Mother and Father) made One, a Many that did not begin united in purpose, as in flavors of social trinitarianism. No, this Many began in a moment in time, meaning that the oneness of God can be seen as a voluntary coming together, a marriage of

---

6 See "To Mrs. [Sylvia Sessions] Lyon" (Trail Diary Version), p. 37.

7 "Apostasy and Restoration," *Ensign*, May 1995, p. 84.

and preservation of Their eternal differences. In this view, no person removed from others or the world is a God; rather, to be a God means to be intimately bound up in relation with others. Hence, Mormon theology ultimately rejects the traditional doctrine of God's impassibility and instead exalts relationality, intimacy, the work of persuasion, and exposure to the Other.

This beginning point of Mormon theology—which Oaks says also represents that theology's "highest aspiration": to make us "like them"[8]—opens other fascinating possibilities. Not the least of these is spirit birth, a concept that, however it works, is bound up in the creative collaboration of Heavenly Mother and Heavenly Father, whose essential differences make Their relationship vital. The belief that we're spirit children of Heavenly Parents alludes to humanity's inherited divine nature; it also points to an eternal push for novelty. Sex differences bring biological value to existence by creating variants of life that may have the superior traits needed to better adapt to and therefore survive in an environment. Vague as the realities of spirit birth may be, we wonder: does Father and Mother's commingling also introduce novelty into existence? Does it fine-tune new lifeforms to an ever-evolving eternal environment? Or does it simply add aesthetic variety and beauty to what otherwise exists in a state of constancy? And on a more basic level, is the universe itself moving toward new varieties of life, new ways of being? Mormon scripture seems to posit that life advances in an ever-repeating cycle—we are

---

8 See also "Becoming Like God," *LDS.org*, February 2014, lds.org/topics/becoming-like-god. Accessed 10 February 2018.

thus only doing what has been done on other worlds. This view holds that every entity inherits a pre-existing type or form that has existed from eternity to eternity. But there is another way of looking at the "eternal round," which sees the reiteration as radical and expansive, spiraling out from its current state and emerging into untapped, unexplored space. In this light, the merging of differences conceives newness. The Son reiterates the image of Father and Mother, but He also becomes something neither Father nor Mother are in and of Themselves.

The concept of Heavenly Mother also opens a more comforting and inclusive notion of eternal family. Mormon theology and religious practices have enshrined the family unit, but have done so by focusing more on creating eternal families through sealings of spouses and of children to parents and less on sealing the individual to the Heavenly Family. For those who are rejected by their earthly families, who are cast off in divorce or by parental neglect, or who are never able to find a companion, Mormonism promises that the faithful can be sealed to Heavenly Parents, that our peers in this world are actual spirit brothers and sisters, and that we can find love, joy, and belonging in the Community of Heaven as the ultimate Family of importance. This may grant a sense of peace and hope to those who struggle with failed or lacking biological and marital relationships. The Church might benefit from putting this notion of Family at the forefront of its teachings on and concerted defense of the family.

These possibilities (and many others) speak to why we felt like we were approaching the holy with this project. Like much religious art, the poems in *Dove Song* contain what Eliza R.

Snow called "a secret something"[9] that points beyond the limits of language. Perhaps best compared to a revelation or a sacrament, art discloses a reality previously absent to observers either because their own imaginations have not or sometimes could not see when left to their own devices. In religious art, this can result in a sense of divine presence. And while no art can portray God in totality, transcendent as deity and all persons are, artworks can invoke a fragment of that dimension through which the power of godliness can be manifest. In the case of this book, the poetry may have the potential to unveil the aspects of God manifest in Heavenly Mother.

We're grateful for the generosity and grace of the poets who contributed work to this volume. Our deepest thanks to them, and to the many others who have had a hand in nurturing and beautifying this project, including the painters who provided art for the anthology's cover and partitions. May readers find sacred sustenance here, among the branching lines of these poems, in the space of these stanzas. May they contemplate Heavenly Mother with a renewed sense of kinship and rejoicing.

---

9 See "Invocation, or the Eternal Father and Mother," p. 35.

INTRODUCTION

SUSAN ELIZABETH HOWE

Before I begin this introduction, I need to bring its limitations to the attention of the reader. In preparing to write it, I typed forty-seven pages of notes, about five times as much discussion and information as my finished text could include. For every claim I make, I had to choose only one or two of many possible poems to illustrate my meaning. My comments will suggest several important contributions *Dove Song* makes and offer a few ideas to consider when reading the poems, but there is so much more to explore in this fine work; the anthology is rich and complex and intricate. The introduction may point you in a few directions, but the revelations and surprises you discover will come from your own passage through the book's pages.

Dove Song is unique in the canon of Mormon literature. And uniquely important. Not only is it a work of fine art, a carefully arranged series of poems that the poets have used their finest skill and training to create, but it is a work of history, a work of inspiration, and a sacred record of many individuals' spiritual quest for additional revealed knowledge about Mother in Heaven.

This collection is of historical importance, particularly in the first section, as it demonstrates that Joseph Smith taught many early Nauvoo saints, including brethren, the doctrine of Mother in Heaven before his death in 1844. We know Eliza R. Snow's great poem "Invocation, or the Eternal Father and Mother," because we sing it several times a year as the lyrics to the hymn "O My Father." But in this anthology that poem is supported by many others written by such leaders as W.W. Phelps, Edward Tullidge, and Orson F. Whitney, all offering evidence that Eliza was not the only person to whom the prophet Joseph taught this doctrine. It is important to read the endnotes in conjunction with each poem; the notes explain both unfamiliar phrases and why the poem matters as a historical document.

I was struck by the authority with which the 19th century poets speak of Mother and Father; they seemed to know and accept the doctrine of Mother in Heaven as a real and present concept of their faith, a logical explanation of why we are male and female on this earth and what our faithful lives may lead to in the eternities. To W.W. Phelps, "the myst'ry that man hath not seen" is "our Father in heaven, and Mother, the Queen." Edward W. Tullidge writes of "the path / That leads to God and the celestial sphere, / Where sexes reach their culminating point, // And Lives eternal send their circles down." There is no hesitancy or questioning in these poems; rather, they rigorously affirm that we have a Mother as well as a Father in Heaven, and that They together exemplify our possible eternal destiny as kings and queens, priests and priestesses of other worlds.

I was surprised that most of these poems attribute the same power and glory to Mother as to Father. They are usually depicted as acting together, often in the traditional roles of parents—nurturing and teaching Their children, bidding them goodbye as they depart for life on Earth or embracing them as they return. Alfred Osmond ascribes equal responsibility to our Heavenly Parents as he prays to both: "Father! Mother! In pity hear my cries! / Grant that thy son, while in this mortal dream! / May not, through sin, break those endearing ties / That bind man to his God and chain the earth and skies." However, some of the poems—especially those near the end of the century—descend into Victorian stereotypes in describing Mother in Heaven. Beauty is the single characteristic mentioned about both Mother in Heaven and her daughters who strive to be like her. Osmond describes Father in Heaven as "a Mighty King" and Mother as a "lovely Queen." Yet, Orson F. Whitney addresses a righteous woman, one he calls "Queen of the future, Eve of coming worlds, / Mother of sun-born myriads yet to be," as "Thou, of beauty loveliest form and phase"; the only characteristic he mentions is not her wisdom, her righteousness, her faith, or her charity, but her beauty. The most egregious example of diminishing our Mother in Heaven to a Victorian stereotype is Charles Edmund Richardson in his epic about the creation. This is how he brings her into the poem: "There came, with seraph step, a form that flits / Through angels' dreams. Lo! Heaven's own loved Queen! / Who seemed to borrow from his brightness, / Till all heaven brighter at Her presence grew." Again, our Heavenly Mother's one characteristic, as usual of women presented in male-authored Victorian works, is her beauty. She apparently has no light of her own; she borrows from Heavenly Father's "brightness." As the poem continues to describe the rebellion of Lucifer and those who follow him, Heavenly Mother is completely passive and unaware of the plan that will provide for the progression and salvation of her children. "Are they lost that have rebelled?" she asks. "May I still hope for them?" But most of the poems create much more equal depictions of Mother and Father in Heaven.

Another curious historical fact that this collection reveals is that Latter-day Saints seem to have written no noteworthy poems about Mother in Heaven between about 1910 and 1973. (Given the editors' rigorous historical investigation, I'm sure that if there had been any such poems, they would have included them.) What accounts for this sudden silence, this turning away from what had been a vibrant Church doctrine? This sixty-year period was the era of standardizing the organization of the Church. It resulted in a clear separation of men's and women's roles and the deference of women to priesthood leaders[10], which may have been factors in limiting women's expression about Mother in Heaven. But these ideas are entirely speculative, unsupported by more than cursory research. Surely the question posed by the lack of poems about Heavenly Mother between 1910 and 1973 deserves additional thought and historical study. Why were such poems no longer written? What was happening with women? with men? with the Church?

Then, in the early 1970s, as the anthology illustrates, there was renewed attention to Mother in Heaven in poetry. But these poems, which are featured in the anthology's second section, were usually more hesitant, sadder; they express a longing for more knowledge about our Heavenly Mother and a yearning for her comfort and guidance. Kristine Rose Barrett

---

10 *The Relief Society Bulletin*, vol. 1, no. 2, February 1914, p. 1.

laments to her Mother, "I think of you often. / I walk along the beach / and do not find your footprints," and Lisa Bolin Hawkins pleads, "I need you, who gave me birth / In your own image, to reveal your ways." Carol Lynn Pearson speaks of the "Motherless house" she lives in and observes, "When I had words enough to ask / 'Where is my Mother?' / No one seemed to know / And no one thought it strange / That no one else knew either." Margaret Rampton Munk compares her adopted daughter's grief at not knowing her birth mother with her own grief at not knowing "one whose memory / My birth erased; / Who let me go / To other parents / Who could train and shape the soul / She had prepared."

Unlike the robust, authoritative 19th century poems, the poems of this later time period contain far more questions than answers. There are questions about Mother's identity: "I want to know your name. / Can you please whisper it to me? / What is your name?" (Kristine Rose Barrett). About her whereabouts: "Where are the ears that first heard me draw breath / when all of infinity listened for every child to squall? / [....] where is it, the heart that sang through my first dreams?" (Marden Clark). Questions about the reasons for Heavenly Mother's silence: "Have I denied you, Mother, unaware? / Have you stretched out your hand, and I not seen?" (Nola Wallace). And questions about her daughters' needs for her guidance: "How can I / become a goddess when the patterns here / Are those of gods?" (Lisa Bolin Hawkins).

In terms of the poems' focus, tone, and attitude, there is a fluidity between the second and third sections of the anthology, but generally speaking, the poems of the third section are more likely to pray directly to Heavenly Mother, to speak honestly about the damage not knowing Her creates for women, and to ask with urgency for more revealed truth. Thalia Pope's "Unspoken Prayer"—the last poem in the collection—does all these things. There is an irony in the title "Unspoken Prayer," given that the poem speaks from the page, if not in an oral iteration. But the title is accurate in that the poem says what women have been prevented from saying, although it is their truth, their real experience. The voice of the poem is an individual woman, probably Pope herself, openly expressing to Heavenly Mother the pain in her heart and life that not knowing her Mother creates. She addresses Mother directly, explaining that, while men "sit, stand, / speak before lemon-oiled pulpits in black / suits, behind temple veils in snow-white ties," Mother and her servants "seem hidden, like naked / blushing skin under cotton-poly cloth." She cries out in pain: "This silence slices and divides, my God, / twists my heart into braided tourniquets." And she asks of her Mother, "Why don't you speak, stand, be seen beside him, / when he reveals himself?" She expresses one discrepancy many women have noted about the temple ceremony: "In Eden, Elohim—a plural name— / commands creation from a single mouth." If Elohim means "the Gods," shouldn't both Mother and Father be depicted? This is a faithful sister, her pleas expressed in "sweepings of slippers / ascending spiral carpet stairs, fragile / turnings and siftings of tissue-papered / scripture sieved between verses," her search "knotted / […] in the reverent rustlings / of pleated robes slipping over shoulders, / in the clinking of plastic thimbles dropped, / empty of water, into trays." She implores, "Command / me, Mother, to wash clean these muddied eyes // and tongue," expressing her great need for vision, clarity, revelation, truth. Even this redaction expresses some of the poem's power; in its entirety it is heartfelt and deeply spiritual.

The other unique aspect of this anthology is that most of the poems it includes record the personal quest of the poets to learn about their Mother in Heaven. One of the first requirements in studying a poem is to determine who the poem's speaker is. It may be a created persona, an invented character who enables the poet to conceal his own attitudes regarding the poem's subject. Or it may be a voice that is very close to the poet's own, a representation of her own thoughts, feelings, and expression. Most of the poems in this collection are the latter type. There are some humorous expressions and a few slick, glib poems that are immediately identifiable by their difference from the others, in tone as well as subject matter, but in most cases, the poets speak sincerely in their own voices about a subject that matters deeply to them—their Mother in Heaven. I would say that these poets have sought and received inspiration through the act of creating the poems, and that the poems are the record of that inspiration. One has to imagine God before coming to any deep confirmation of who God is; in this case the God the poets hope to learn of is God the Mother.

Braided through the book are several tropes used to arrive at such inspiration. One is the use of imagery associated with conceiving, carrying, and giving birth to a child. Marden Clark writes of "The womb that sheltered me when every part was potential, / that tent [...] that held me against the vacuum, / that cradled me in the bowels of mercy, sheltered." Melody Newey Johnson imagines herself as a nursing infant: "I miss her breast today; / her heart, pulsing / against my cheek," concluding the poem by explaining the absence of Mother: "She is weaning me and / I am weeping mother's milk." "The Milk of the Mother" is the title of Alex Caldiero's vibrant poem that creates metaphors of power for Mother's milk: it is "born from the heart's fire / and makes of love a brilliant sun"; it is "distilled in the stars / and pours with the light of dawn." Rachel Hunt Steenblik relates a woman's postpartum sorrow to her Heavenly Mother's: after the work of creating the world, "the Mother knew / sorrow—the emptiness / that comes after fullness, / the softness that remains / for a long time."

Like Steenblik's poem, one of the strategies of imagining Mother in Heaven is to bring her into situations faced by contemporary women, especially situations in which they need comfort and support. Taylor Rouanzion's refrain, "A mother's pain / Needs a Mother's comfort," seems to have been a prompt for many poems. Rouanzion's own poem portrays several women who need their Heavenly Mother's love and blessing, including one who has been unable to conceive and one who fears that her inability to teach her children correct principles is the cause of their difficult lives. Deja Early writes of her delivery of a very premature baby at home, and of thinking, "as we drive to the hospital, // of Mother in Heaven, wondering whether / half-organized souls ever dissipated, / split from her without warning, / left her in grief." In Rebekah Orton's poem, "Heavenly Mother Eats Carbs," the speaker hates her body, given "the weight of years and children." But just as she turns away from the mirror, she says, "I glimpse her in my widened hips, / my deflated breasts, / the silver purple lines that map my abdomen: / a sense of power etched across my veins." In another poem, "It's Possible I'm Projecting," Orton imagines that Mother in Heaven has the same problems as a mortal mother of stubborn and needy toddlers.

Along with these tropes of childbirth and maternal struggle, the anthology features imagery of Mother Earth. The connection of Mother Earth with the Goddess has a long history, although the ancient goddess Gaia of Greek mythology, who actually was Mother Earth and created herself out of primordial chaos, is not comparable to Mother in Heaven as Mormons understand Her. Nevertheless, many poets in this anthology have made the connection between Mother in Heaven and some aspect of the natural world. Kristine Rose Barrett addresses Heavenly Mother thus: "I see the stars and think / I see strung diamonds plaited / in your hair." Melody Newey Johnson writes of missing Mother in Heaven, except that sometimes, "in the mountains," she thinks she hears "an echo // of the flute" Mother plays. Robert Rees assumes the voice of Mother in Heaven saying, "I ride on the backs / of dolphins and unicorns. / I am the wings of doves, / the feathers of / superb lyrebirds, / the wild call of / ivory-billed woodpeckers." There are many poems in this vein, most of them creating metaphors for Mother in Heaven.

The use of metaphor is a particularly effective technique for engaging the reader in the attempt to imagine Mother in Heaven, because the reader has to participate in determining the meaning of the metaphor. For example, in Tina Lindsay's poem, "My Mother Is ...," each stanza claims something different about who Mother is: ocean, earth, moon, shadow, me. The first stanza says, "My mother is the ocean— / The color of an eye, edged in foamy lace. / She is an equal partner to heaven— / As she negotiates rainfall with the sky." The metaphor Lindsay employs compares Heavenly Mother to the ocean. But what about Mother in Heaven is like the ocean? While the lines that follow the metaphor offer Lindsay's answers, the reader is first invited to consider the metaphor personally and come up with his/her own explanations. Before reading mine, think of this question for yourself: why do you think Mother in Heaven is like the ocean? In other words, create your own meaning for the metaphor. There are so many possibilities: both Mother in Heaven and the ocean are the source of life on Earth; both are vast, have great depth, and cannot be fully conceived by humans; both have immense power; both can be punishing at some times and comforting at others. Lindsay's lines offer more connections between oceans and Heavenly Mother, and these connections hint at others, in a long chain of recognition. Metaphor is a particularly important literary exercise in the search for Mother in Heaven because sincere effort in attempting to understand Mother, when combined with prayer and the emulation of her immense love and goodness, will lead to additional inspiration about who She is.

The LDS canon of scripture includes no direct, individual revelation of our Heavenly Mother. Given that fact, it is a particularly bold act to imagine and speak in her voice, as several poems do. She says, in S.E. Page's poem, "Utter it even to the end of the earth," that "I will not keep silence— / The time of the singing of birds is come. / Behold, thy mother! Even from the beginning. / Set me as a seal upon thine heart." Robert A. Rees' poem "Mother" has her say, "I am. / I exist. / Not somewhere. / Not in silence. / But there, / in the hollows / of your heart, / in your veins / and blood and cells, / in your deepest memory, / I am there." And in Cheryl Bruno's "Message to Cecily," Heavenly Mother delivers the message, the first stanza of which says, "A great loneliness has now descended: / Within you there is a space that yearns, / A heart-hollow—to teach you to return / And to watch for Me, which I have intended." I would direct you to read the whole poem, which is wise and lovely.

I would like to conclude by noting what a great gift this anthology will be for many LDS people, particularly for many women. Everyone has a story of her need for Mother in Heaven. Mine is related to the death of my own mother. At that time, I felt a clear witness that my mother was passing into another realm, not ceasing to exist, but I was suddenly brought to a blankness in trying to understand where she might be now, what she might be doing, and what her eternal future might be. A woman who loved others as my mother did should have a challenging and exciting assignment in the eternities. She should share in the work of our Mother in Heaven. But we know almost nothing about Mother in Heaven's work, power, or identity. While we can infer much about Her character and actions as a result of Her divinity, we don't know what her role was in the premortal existence, how she participates in the plan of salvation, or how she interacts with her children during their mortal existence.

We don't know because little about our Mother in Heaven has been revealed. "Truth is reason," said Eliza R. Snow, and reason tells me that women, having gifts that are similar to men's, having agency and integrity, and having served and sacrificed for others, deserve to know their worth and eternal potential. Women have been denied the truth they need to understand the eternal promises of God to them, not because God considers them secondary and inferior and plans for them to do nothing but give birth to spirits eternally, but because we haven't asked for additional revelation about our Mother. As the ninth Article of Faith claims, we believe that there are many great and important things yet to be revealed concerning the kingdom of God, which things must surely include a revelation of the identity, eternal work, and power of God the Mother and her eternal daughters.

A study of the history of the Church demonstrates that most often revelation comes as people prepare themselves for it, and as leaders humbly come before God and pray for answers to burning questions. In my opinion, this anthology is of tremendous importance in helping to create the discussion that will prepare us for a revelation of our Eternal Mother, and in demonstrating that women's questions are, in our dispensation, the burning questions that need to be answered.

PART ONE

A Mother There

1844 – 1910

A Song of Zion

How sweet is the communion
Of saints that fear the Lord,
And strive, in perfect union,
To gain the great reward.
'Tis like the oil on Aaron
Anointing him a priest,
Perfumed with rose from Sharon,
And Cassia from the east.

'Tis like the dew of Hermon,
Where God began to bless,
And promised in his sermon,
Eternal happiness.
'Tis like the precious ointment
That God Almighty had
At Jesus Christ's appointment,
Which made his heart so glad.

'Tis like a little leaven
The woman hid for good,
When she, as queen of heaven,
In gold of Ophir stood.
'Tis like the court of Zion,
Where garments all are white;
Who'll reign like Judah's Lion,
In everlasting light.

Their robes alike in beauty,
Their hearts and faith agree,
They'll ever be on duty
Till all their race is free,
They'll eat the hidden manna,
Receive the precious stone,
And sing the great hosanna
Where God and Christ are one.

[1844]

A Voice from the Prophet: Come to Me

Come to me, will ye come to the saints that have died,—
To the next better world, where the righteous reside;
Where the angels and spirits in harmony be
In the joys of a vast Paradise? Come to me.

Come to me where the truth and the virtues prevail;
Where the union is one, and the years never fail;
Where a heart can't conceive, nor a nat'ral eye see,
What the Lord has prepar'd for the just: Come to me.

Come to me where there is no destruction or war;
Neither tyrants, or mobbers, or nations ajar;
Where the system is perfect, and happiness free,
And the life is eternal with God: Come to me.

Come to me, will ye come to the mansion above,
Where the bliss and the knowledge, the light, and the love,
And the glory of God, do eternally be?
Death, the wages of sin, is not here: Come to me.

Come to me, here are Adam and Eve at the head
Of a multitude, quicken'd and rais'd from the dead;
Here's the knowledge that was, or that is, or will be—
In the gen'ral assembly of worlds: Come to me.

Come to me, here's the myst'ry that man hath not seen;
Here's our Father in heaven, and Mother, the Queen;
Here are worlds that have been, and the worlds yet to be,
Here's eternity,—endless; amen: Come to me.

Come to me all ye faithful and blest of Nauvoo:
Come ye Twelve, and ye High Priests, and Seventies, too;
Come ye Elders, and all of the great company;—
When you've finish'd your work on the earth: Come to me.

Come to me; here's the future, the present and past:
Here is Alpha, Omega, the first and the last;
Here's the fountain, the "river of life," and the Tree;
Here's your Prophet & Seer, Joseph Smith: Come to me.

[1845]

Invocation, or
the Eternal Father and Mother

O my Father, thou that dwellest
In the high and glorious place;
When shall I regain thy presence,
And again behold thy face?
In thy holy habitation,
Did my spirit once reside?
In my first primeval childhood
Was I nurtur'd near thy side?

For a wise and glorious purpose
Thou hast plac'd me here on earth,
And withheld the recollection
Of my former friends and birth;
Yet oft times a secret something
Whispered you're a stranger here;
And I felt that I had wandered
From a more exalted sphere.

I had learned to call thee father,
Through thy Spirit from on high,
But, until the key of knowledge
Was restor'd, I knew not why.
In the heav'ns are parents single?
No, the thought makes reason stare;
Truth is reason—truth eternal
Tells me I've a mother there.

When I leave this frail existence—
When I lay this mortal by,
Father, mother, may I meet you
In your royal courts on high?
Then, at length, when I've completed
All you sent me forth to do,
With your mutual approbation
Let me come and dwell with you.

[1845]

Excerpt from
"To Mrs. [Sylvia Sessions] Lyon"
(Trail Diary Version)

And the Saints of God who're banished
From their country and their home,
Who, for Jesus' testimony
In the wilderness now roam,
Will with pray'r and supplication
Plead for thee before the throne
Of the great eternal mother,
Do not feel thyself alone.

[1847]

Epistle—
Inscribed to S. R. [Sarah Richards]

Dear sister, though few days have past
Since you and I have met,
I feel our friendship still will last
When Time's last sun is set.

For oh! what can that love destroy
Which dwelt with us of yore,
When in our Father's blest employ
We His bright image bore.

And now, made one by Truth on earth,
We feel the kindling flame
Which gave our spirits former birth,
A parentage, and name;

And will in after worlds resume
A higher glory far,
Where Kings and Priests immortal bloom,
And God's dominions are.

Yes! then we'll see our Father's face,
As formerly we've seen,
And feel a mother's fond embrace,
And know what we have been;

And how our elder brother was
The first-begotten Son,
And kept his Father's Heavenly laws,
And life eternal won!

And how that love which fired his breast,
Shall us inspire the same;
That we like him may gain that rest,
Through whom we have a claim;

That all our kindred spirits may
Return again to God,
Through substitution's thorny way,
Who kept their first abode.

Then let us keep by firm resolve,
The cov'nant we have made;
Nor let temptation ere dissolve
What God in Truth hath said.

Yes, sister, if you steadfast prove,
And be as you have been,
You'll wear a crown in Heaven above,
And reign on earth a queen!

[1853]

Marriage

Geminous universe! Creation's twins!
What loving proneness, every where disclosed
Throughout existence, for a double self;
Two lives, two natures, and two kindred souls,
That form the One, and Being make complete:—
They are but parts, and not two perfect wholes.
Great Nature, in her generative course,
Moulds all her works in halves.
Man is imperfect when without his mate;
Nor can they separate travel up the path
That leads to God and the celestial sphere,
Where sexes reach their culminating point,

And Lives eternal send their circles down.
On every page where the Creative power
Hath wrote its wondrous genesis of life,
These great relations God and Truth maintain;
Nor hints that He will ever sexes end.
How vain his laws, how meaningless His works,
If into non-descriptive chaos we
Should be resolved, when at perfection's stage;

Not male nor female, father, mother, child,
Nor wife, nor husband, brother, sister, kin!
But can perfection those relations end,
On which it builds itself and travels up?
Or is that Being who by sexes works—
Made a Creator by creation's scheme—
Himself a sexless and non-mated God?
A "perfect" man and yet himself no man?
His works on earth, but pattern things above;
And family ties run through the Godly state,
And holy marriage leads to "Endless Lives."

Dear brother, sister, mated first in love,
It whispered each had found this second self!
Two kindred souls, two hearts, with fondness mov'd,
You entered wedlock, God hath made you One.
Keep strong those ties, give love eternal youth,
Nor e'er be parted whom the Lord hath joined.
So shall you be like the first holy pair,
Who once in Eden were each other's worlds,
Till you be parents of a race as great.

[1857]

Our Existence—
Past, Present, and Future

Oh, we've been, yes, we've been in a bright world before,
Where we liv'd with our Father and Mother of yore;
And they nurs'd us as those that were tender and fair,
And wreath'd with fresh flow'rets our beautiful hair.

Oh, the streamlets which flow'd thro' those gardens above,
Were clear as the crystal of Ed'ns first love;
And the songs that we sang were all noble and true
As the palm trees of Heaven that over us grew.

But how many we were, and how boundless our bliss,
We cannot unfold in such regions as this;
For the vail hath come down o'er that landscape of light,
And now we are left in the shadows of night.

So our garments are chang'd and our glory hath fled,
And the sackcloth is ours and dust on our head;
And our Father and Mother are hidden on high,
And the storm-clouds are black in the wint'ry sky.

Yet we'll quickly return to the mansions of light,
Resplendent again in our garments of white;
And the face of our Father shall smile in that morn,
When the bands of the grave, asunder are torn.

So we'll tread the fair scenes that we've trodden before,
With honor surpassing the ages of yore,
While the friends that have clustered like kingdoms around,
Shall then in our trains with their glories be found.

And thou, Father, for ever in splendor shalt shine,
And we'll toil, toil, toil for a glory like thine,
And the palm trees shall wave and clear streamlets flow,
Which we left in our Eden to wander below.

[1857]

Excerpts from "Songs of the Heart"

O, what songs of the heart
 We shall sing all the day,
When again we assemble at home;
 When we meet ne'er to part,
 With the blest o'er the way,
There no more from our loved ones to roam!

 When we meet ne'er to part,
 O, what songs of the heart
We shall sing in our beautiful home.

~

O, what songs we'll employ!
 O, what welcomes we'll hear!
While our transports of love are complete;
 As the heart swells with joy
 In embraces most dear,
When our heavenly parents we meet,

 As the heart swells with joy,
 O, what songs we'll employ,
When our heavenly parents we meet!

[1879]

What is Life?

There are, who deem life's lingering durance
Designed for freedom and delight;
Its clanking fetters claim as music,
Its darkness worship as 'twere light.

Nor mindful still of loftier purpose,
Vain pleasure's winged flight pursue;
Their dream: "To-day; there comes no morrow"—
That tinkling lie with sound so true.

Was such the charm whose soft alluring
Drew spirits bright from heavenly bliss?
Did morning stars hymn loud hosannas
O'er false and fatal theme like this?

Speak thou, my soul, that once did mingle
Where souls were never doomed to die;
Would worlds on worlds like this have won thee
From glorious realms yet glittering high,

Where Father, Mother, friends, forsaken
Till time their hundred-fold restore.
Await to hail thy welcome coming
When time and trial are no more?

Self-exiled from yon realms supernal,
Obedient to Omniscient rule,
Hiedst here to chase life's fleeting phantoms,
A truant in Time's precious school?

Son of a God, 'mid scenes celestial,
Fellst thou from freedom to be free?
Or, hoping rise of endless raptures.
For time renounced Eternity?

O blindness dense, delusion mortal!
Where darkness reigns disguised as day.
Where prison seems but sportive playground,
And spendthrifts waste life's pearls away!

Be this their bourn that seek no brighter.
Whom naught save worldly pleasures please;
Graves are the goal of earthly glory.
But man was meant for none of these.

Call earth thy home, clasp thou its shadows,
Till here thy little day be done;
My home is where the starry kingdoms
Roll round the Kingdom of the Sun!

I came not forth in quest of freedom,
To shrink from peril or from pain;
To learn from death life's deepest lessons,
I sank to rise, I serve to reign.

'Tis contrast sways unceasing sceptre
O'er vast appreciation's realm,
E'en Gods, through sacrifice descending.
Triumphant rise to overwhelm.

Thus fetters teach the force of freedom,
Thus sickness, joys of future health,
Thus folly's fate proves wisdom's warning.
Thus poverty prepares for wealth.

Souls to whom life unfolds its meaning,
Ne'er hope full happiness on earth,
But patient bide that brighter morrow
Which brings again celestial birth.

[1882]

Excerpts from
Elias: An Epic of the Ages

Thou, of beauty loveliest form and phase,
Goddess dethroned, divinity uncrowned,
Partner and peer of human majesty!
Sharing with him life's jointed sovereignty,
Well canst thou wait for thrones and diadems.
Queen of the future, Eve of coming worlds,
Mother of sun-born myriads yet to be,
Spirits resplendent that shall people stars,
And hail thee empress of a universe!

~

Ever with them, earth-wandering Witnesses,
The heralds of a kingdom yet to come,
Kingdom upon and yet not of the earth,
Whose portal none can enter, none can see,
Save born anew, born of a dual birth,
By mystic fatherhood and motherhood
Begotten sons and daughters unto God.

~

Man a divinity in embryo,
Who, ere he reign above, must serve below;
His spirit in earth element baptize;
For birth, as death, a baptism to the wise.
The gulf that parts the lower from the higher
Bridged by development of son to Sire,
Of daughter unto Mother's high estate;
For e'en as man's, the woman's future fate.

As sun, or moon, or varying star, appears
Each heir of glory in those endless spheres,
God's grace condoning life's unpaid arrears.

~

Spirit and body, blending, make the soul,
As halves, uniting, form the perfect whole;
Symbol of wedded bliss, celestial state,
The sealing of the sexes, mate to mate,
That heirs with Christ may reign as queens and kings
Where endless union endless increase brings;
Where souls a sweet affinity shall find,
And restitution's edict seal and bind
Eternal matter to eternal mind;
Like unto like, for night weds not with day,
And Order's mandate e'en the Gods obey.

Where blest in heaven, though curst in earth and hell,
The law that framed the house of Israel,
Light's lineal sheath and faith's fraternity,
The called and chosen of eternity;
Where lives, ne'er ending lives, perpetuate
The joys, a myriad-fold, of mortal state,
And bind with links welded in lesser years
The love-united systems of the spheres.

The body as the sheath without the sword;
No man without the woman in the Lord;
Each pair the Eve and Adam of some world,
Perchance unborn, unorbited, unwhirled.

[1904]

To Unseen Friends

Though on earth we've had no meeting,
Still I send you words of greeting
That may stir our souls with echoes
      From that far-off seraph shore;
Ere we left golden portals
Of the home of the immortals,
Where in our primeval childhood,
      Sported we in days of yore.

Here the sorrowing, heavy-laden
Still by faith may see that aiden
Where the good and true the victory
      Shall joy forevermore.
What though clouds and storms surround us
Though in darkness they have bound us,
Yet we know the sun is shining
      High above the tempest roar.

Thus my heart seems sometimes swelling,
With a joy beyond all telling;
As though in my memory lingered,
      Echoes of that golden shore—
Telling of the waves of gladness,
Ere our hearts were stung with sadness,
Ere we left our parents' mansion,
      Or these mortal forms we wore.

O, my distant friends and brothers,
We are each and all another's,
And the heart that gives most freely
     From its treasure hath the more;
For in giving love we find it,
With a golden chain we bind it,
Like an amulet of safety
     To our hearts for evermore.

[1886]

Excerpt from "Thoughts on Death"

This life is like a summer evening's dream;
We now are here, but long we cannot stay.
E'en as a leaf that's thrown in yonder stream,
And toward the ocean is fast borne away;
So we, like leaves, upon life's stream do play.
Our efforts weak can never stay the tide.
Whe'er tossed and tumbled by the surging spray,
Or smoothly o'er its glassy surface glide,
Time's stream still bears us on toward that ocean wide.

The sun of life, with golden rays of light,
Now shines on him whose youthful hand
Doth trace these lines; but soon death's clouds of night
Will gather o'er his head, and then no place
Can e'er be found upon this world's broad face
Where friend or foe will meet with him again:
But somewhere in the realms of boundless space
He still shall live, for life cannot be slain.
Immortal is the soul; o'er all things it shall reign.

I dare not love, with all the power of love,
A being that these mortal eyes have seen;
But in those realms of bliss, far, far above,
There reign a Mighty King and lovely Queen.
With them I know my burning soul has been.
Father! Mother! in pity hear my cries!
Grant that thy son, while in this mortal dream!
May not, through sin, break those endearing ties
That bind man to his God and chain the earth and skies.

Far sooner would I hear Death Angel's call
Than see that form, in whate'er shape it came,
Approach that e'en could cause my spirit's fall,
And rob me of that hoped-for place and name.
'Tis far beyond the crumbling peaks of fame!
Where cowering Guilt will hang his head in shame.
E'en on the banks of these Elysian streams,
Where my soul roamed in youth and mused on glorious themes.

[1891]

CHARLES EDMUND RICHARDSON

Excerpts from
Footprints of Gospel Feet
for the Modest-in-Heart

Ante-Principia
    Chapter I

Divine, eternal goodness, let me sing
And bring its light to view of erring man,
That he, perchance, may better understand
The wisdom of the Source from whence we sprang.
And while I sing a theme so great, so grand,
Let me pronounce those sacred names with awe:
With reverential tread let me draw near
The majesty of God and His great Son.

              ~

At dawn of heaven's most eventful day,
Within the inner court of hope's bright home,
Where glory shed its brightest ray divine,
Where hallowed notes of love's sweet music thrilled
And breathed its sacred welcome on the air,
Stood waiting heaven's King. Lo! grace and peace
Beamed from His presence. He it was of whom
The angels sing this song in chorus grand:

He is our Father. From His hand
The seasons roll, the years are sown,
Beneath His eye all creatures stand,
His ear can hear the humblest moan.

In Him His children may confide,
His love leaps over time and space,
O'er all their sorrows He has sighed;
But mercy may not all erase.

For we must suffer to be meek,
Must sorrow ere we willing be.
Must feel despair ere we will seek
To conquer pride, or bow the knee.

Then Hail to wisdom, might and love
Whose lustre ages cannot dim!
Give praise to Him who reigns above.
He is our Father. Hail to Him!

Alone; He waited for a coming One,
While He whose frown could crush the universe,
Now wore a sad, sweet smile. Thus some great cloud
When tinged with glory by the setting sun,
So seems to smile despite its present loss,
In hope of a more glorious to-morrow.
For Him a sun of dearly cherished hope
Was setting even then; but wisdom His
To make His secret purposes bring forth
For other days and times. Anon He knew
The coming sad of One He loved indeed,

And nearer as in haste that loved One came,
That holy music breathed a tinge of pain,
And consolation trembled on His lips,
And vied with rapture to be first to greet.
There came, with seraph step, a form that flits
Through angels' dreams. Lo! Heaven's own loved Queen!
Who seemed to borrow from His brightness,
till All heaven brighter at Her presence grew.
Of Her the angels sing in chorus sweet:

> She is our Mother. From Her hand
> We took the joys of former youth;
> She taught our childhood precepts grand,
> And guided in the ways of truth.
>
> Sweet pity dwells within Her breast,
> And leaps forth at Her children's wail;
> The sin-sick soul will there find rest.
> And love whose depth will never fail.
>
> Her trust sublime in Father wise,
> Is deathless as eternity;
> O let Her children all arise.
> And bless Her proud maternity.
>
> Then Hail to pity, love and trust,
> That to His will makes no demur!
> O, give Her love and praise; 'tis just;
> She is our mother. Hail to Her!

Then spake their eyes, a holy joy undimmed
By that great sorrow welling from their hearts.
While thus our Mother in grief-stricken tones:
"O Thou in whom my trust alway abides!
Canst thou some grain of comfort give me now?
Our children! Are they lost that have rebelled?
Tumultuous they cavil at thy will,
Inveigh against the wisdom that agreed
On some wise law in council yesterday.

O, blind indeed are they, and hard of heart
Who cannot see in Thee omnipotence
Twined with affection, pure, and deep and strong.
And guided by rich wisdom on its way.

O, how could they so soon forget the past,
The tender, loving, soul-endearing past,
Whose legion voices whisper duty's way.
May I still hope for them?"
                              Then spake our God:
"O Thou Eternal Fountain of my joy!
Be comforted! for never shall the soul
Be fully lost, that wishes to be saved.
How often has thy Mother's love remarked:
'Our children are not even two alike!'
Some worthy are of station like to ours,
While some must taste of horrible despair
Ere their proud souls will heed our second law.
Obedience, (by which we all are here;)
And some perhaps must go to punishment
Far worse than death, till sin has made amends.

You know we had with one accord agreed
That first-born Jesus worthy is to reign
O'er that new earth, where we their souls will prove.
While yesterday we counseled o'er the plan,
There came proud Lucifer, our wayward son,
To ask that he be granted that high place,
For that he would save more; would all men save;
Explaining that he would mankind compel,
To yield obedience to him and right.
I then anew unfolded to his mind
That first eternal law, whereby all souls,
Are free to do their will with their own selves.
Like blazing meteor across the sky,
Our son shot from my presence full of wrath.
We then decreed, through his deep rage and hate,
To try our children in their first estate;
Withdraw my spirit's counsels from them till
He tempt them; that the proud might fall and not
Have glory in that Kingdom with the meek;
And as there must be opposition fierce,
To prove the nobler ones among the just.
We will let those who fall oppose the right
While that new earth is peopled with our race.
Thus, while they think to mar the holy plan.
Their ire shall only further Justice'[s] ends.
Grieve not for them, for they are In my hands;
Instead, rejoice in these dear, faithful ones,
Who dire ordeal now bravely, nobly, pass;
For once my spirit quite forsakes the mind,
Hell's tortures enter in; bright hope takes wings;
Wild doubt and dread despair by turns enslave:

Then only innate goodness can resist
That guile, whose flattery and sophistry can please,
But Jesus comes. To-day will further try
This faithful host, that each his worth may prove."
While thus in holy love their souls communed,
A being came, and knelt before them there,
Who seemed the very image of the King.
Of Him the angels sing in chorus glad:

> He is our Brother. From His hand
> Were dropped our blessings while on earth;
> His care fills all the teeming land,
> Regardless of man's faith or worth.

> But when in faith man seeks His truth.
> Then joy is His all doubt to chase,
> And blessings add; for all He doeth
> Is for the welfare of our race.

> His meekness triumphed over sin,
> His grace disarmed death's agony,
> His truth the Gospel brings us in.
> To heaven's immortality.

> Then Hail to meekness, truth, and grace!
> Praise them all tongues in sacred hymn;
> And trust in Him who saves our race;
> He is our brother. Hail to Him!

Then as He knelt and raised a wan, sad face
That lacked the lustre it was wont to wear;
That voice that now can all earth's creatures thrill,
Thus faltered forth; "My Father and my God
Why hast Thou thus forsaken us?" To which
The Father's own soul-healing tones replied:
"For your eternal good, my well-beloved.
Till now my children knew not their own selves,
Much less the Holy Spirit's aid and worth.
Then how could they this precious knowledge gain,
Except an hour of weighty trial came,
Wherein their souls deprived of my support
Might learn its worth, and their own course decide,
Nor could my love exempt one single son;
For God must first, all equal trial give.
And as so nobly Thou hast borne the test,
Stand Thou at my right hand, by right and tell
Thy Mother what has lately come to pass;
But first receive anew the Spirit's seal;"
And laid His hand upon that meek bowed head.
Then blazed transcendent glory 'round the brow
Of Him who God delights to own and bless;
Then lighted that mild eye anew with joy,
And grateful words thanked Him who chastens,
that He may more fully, further, teach and bless.
While glowed that face and form again a God's.
Past then the first few moments of new bliss,
Obedient the Son told o'er that fall:
"While yester-eve we joyed in happy throng,
Unmindful of the Comforter, the source
Of all the pleasure beings may receive;

A sudden dread assailed, each sense was seized,
A world of doubt burst into every soul,
Unthought of care oppressed the sinking mind,
And Thou and home seemed endless way removed.
I shuddered when I saw another's face,
For there sat throned grim, hideous despair.
No more my brothers seemed like Father here.
No more my sisters minded me of Thee.
It seemed as if fell darkness chained the soul,
And new and wild impulses drowned the will.
Then Lucifer, our brother, came with news.
On which he dwelt in eloquent harangue.
He said it had just been decreed that all
Who will not do just so, while on the earth,
Will be condemned, and may not be reclaimed;
That all must risk eternal weal or woe
Dependent on the grace and worth of one,
Whom all know is no better than the rest;
That such dependence is unfit for souls
Of beings so intelligent as we;
And that we must unite in firm demand
That glory be not wrested from the host,
And heaped upon the head of one so frail.
Then I, in sorrow, begged him to desist,
And heed his every word would wound the soul
Of Him whose laws could never be unjust;
And further I would have persuaded him,
But some he had already deftly won;
These drowned my voice with hisses, cries and groans.
And clamored that he should be heard—speak on.
Then as he spoke, light seemed to darkness turn.
And darkness seemed the light, for right looked wrong;

And only they that loved the Father more
Than their own selves, are faithful from that hour.
One-third, afflicted by their own sad state,
Lamenting some, the loss of that proud host,
Do still await the Father's holy will.
With them I had yet been, but that a gleam—
A breath faint whispered 'Come', and I am here.
O Father! may they not, like me, receive
Sure recompense for all they suffer, soon?"
Then answered God: "Thine soon shall be the joy
To lift them from despondency to bliss;
But first, bear Thou my Word to band and flock.
Say to that fallen band; 'Unless they yield
No body shall be born for them on earth.'
When they refuse; say to my faithful flock,
'It is my Will that all who love my name,
Shall now in might contend with Pride's array;
Wield those eternal weapons bright and strong
Of which they know the use; and I will bless.'
Nor is it needless strife, for be there not
A further trial, none will be content
With other than the highest lot on earth;
But lest the trial be too long and harsh.
Take Thou the Holy Spirit's Power great,
With which I now invest Thee, and prepare,
When time is ripe, to overthrow and hurl
Rebellion into outer darkness far.
To place of torment which we will call Hell.
Take from them all their joys and hopes save one.
That of persuading more to join their ranks
While on the earth. We will unseen be near,
To mark those valiant in defense of right;

For they shall be God's servants on the earth."
Then swiftly on His mission sped the Son.

Chapter II

~

When in its noonday splendor blazing high,
Shone He who came, and sweetly smiled on these,
With smile that fell like summer dew on flowers;
But when He turned to them. His frown was terrible.
Low cowered they while thus He spake: "Ye who
Have chosen to rebel against our God!
Bethink ye, how our Mother strove to teach
Her every child, that true obedience.
The source of every dignity and power.
Can ye so soon those God-like truths forget?
Go, then, until despair shall teach anew;
Vessels of wrath, hence! to your torment long."
As autumn leaves before the dread cyclone,
Or Arab sands when hot simoon whirls past,
So were they swept away, and reader, you
In vain looked round for foes, for they were not.

~

[1891]

Our Mother in Heaven

Oh my Mother, thou that dwellest
In thy mansions up on high,
Oft methinks I still remember
How you bade your child goodbye;
How you clasped me to your bosom,
Bade me a true son to be
E're I left my Father's mansion,
To dwell in mortality.

How you gave me words of counsel
To guide aright my straying feet;
How you taught by true example
All of Father's laws to keep;
While I strive in this probation,
How to learn the gospel truth,
May I merit your approval
As I did in early youth.

'Tis recorded in your journal
How you stood by Father's side,
When by pow'rs that are eternal
Thou wast sealed His goddess bride.
How by love and truth and virtue,
E'en in time thou did'st become,
Through your high exalted station,
Mother of the souls of men.

When of evil I've repented,
And my work on earth is done,
Kindest Father, loving mother,
Pray forgive your erring son.
When my pilgrimage is ended,
And the victor's wreath I've won,
Dearest Mother, to your bosom
Will you welcome home your son?

[1892]

A Thread of Thought

My thoughts flew back like a shuttle,
To our first known record of time;
And looping that time with the present,
I have woven them into rhyme.

When the Morning Stars together
Sang out their joyous praise,
And the new, bright Sun, in splendor,
Sent forth its cheering rays;
Dispelling the night's cool vapors,
And chasing the clouds away;
That the evening and the morning,
Might complete the grand First Day.

We were there, with God, our Father,
And voted "Thy will be done,"
And our Mother, Queen in Heaven,
Smiled on us every one,
Smiled on each Eve, each Sarah,
Rachel, Rebecca and Ruth,
Elizabeth, Mary and Martha,
Each daughter that stood for truth.

We were *all* ALL there, my sisters;
And we loved each other well;
And doubtless selected classmates,

With whom upon earth to dwell.
And our Father marked the course
For each and we all accepted,
Nothing was done by force.

We can think how some of us, gazing
Down the long, long line of years,
Had sufficient faith and courage
To enter as volunteers.
While others, afraid of their weakness,
And by earth's strange shadows appalled,
Longed to follow, and yet concluded
To wait till their names were called.

And some even then with a shudder,
Held fast to the Gracious Hand,
And asked, "Shall I have power,
On those slippery heights to stand?
Can you really trust me, Father,
And shall I be strong enough,
To carry those heavy burdens
O'er places so dark and rough?

And our Father, in loving pity,
Answered "Your guides shall bring
Your message to me always,
And I'll help you in everything.
Never forget, my daughter,
That sacred pass word, *prayer*;
Keep it always within your bosom,
And whisper it everywhere."

Well here we are, my sisters,
In the classes we came to fill;
Learning our daily lessons,
Doing our Father's will.
He will clasp our hands with welcomes,
When the mystic veil is drawn,
And as conquerors we enter,
Where we hailed the First Great Dawn.

[1892]

A Welcome

Of all the sweet, endearing words,
Poured forth like music of the birds,
From hearts that sing and souls that pray,
In unison, along the way,
Where helpful, gen'rous acts of love,
Make earth akin to heaven above,
The glad word welcome, is among
The kindest that can grace the tongue.

And this kind word we speak to you,
Our sister-workers, friends most true,
We welcome you with feelings warm,
Which hold no studied, worldly form;
For, like the "lambs" we're called to feed,
Whose law is love's pure, simple creed,
Our hearts o'erflow—each happy face
We'd kiss, and each loved form embrace.

We know your constancy and care,
The heavy burdens you must bear;
How prayerfully you work to win
Christ's little ones from ways of sin;
Your struggles great we realize,
Your strong, true faith we highly prize;
You have supported our best aims;
Our gratitude, your goodness claims.

While all this we appreciate,
Not farther to elaborate,
A little while we will discard
All weary thoughts of labors hard;
And count this hour a time of rest,
Of peace and joy, divinely blest.
Perhaps, we may not all appear,
Together thus another year.

For Zion's Stakes are spreading wide,
New ones are formed, old ones divide;
So we, who have together striv'n,
And our united efforts giv'n,
May soon be called to other ways;
Which matters not, if all our days
Are still devoted to such moves
As God directs and heaven approves.

Let us be grateful for this day,
Rejoice together while we may;
Praise God for prophets as of old,
His revelations to unfold;
And holy women who have stood
The grandest tests of womanhood;
Thank Him that we may follow on,
Where many noble ones have gone.

Such gatherings as this, perchance,
Are harbingers, which in advance,
Give foretastes of immortal bliss,
Of Father's blessing, Mother's kiss,
In that fair home, to which we all
Shall one day gather, at Their call;
And where each faithful child will find
A loving welcome, glad and kind.

[1899]

C. C. A. CHRISTENSEN

Et aandeligt Lysbillede

Naar Solen sig sænker og spreder sit Skær
Af Guld over Mark, over Blomster og Trær—
Og Bjergenes Toppe samt Skyernes Rand,
Forgyldt sig afspejler i Søernes Vand;
Da ser jeg bag Skyen et Glimt af mit Hjem,
Og Tanker om Himlen vil trænge sig frem.

Jeg synes mig hensat i Himlen hos Gud,
Og hører ham udstede Almagts Bud:
„Bliv Lys!"—Og af Kaos en Verden ud sprang,
Som hver i sin Orden han satte i Gang.
Jeg syntes at høre Guds Sønner i Kor,
Med Jubel velsigne den nyskabte Jord.

En Bolig for Menneskets Slægt var beredt—
Og Adam som Stamfader dertil udset,
Den første af alle, den ældste paa Jord—
„Den gamle af Dage" ifølge Guds Ord—
Af Gudernes Slægt og en himmelsk Monark,
Han var, og vil være, vor Slægts Patriark.

Og Kvinden—en Datter af Eva, vor Mo'r
Blev Frelserens Moder paa denne vor Jord.
Den Højestes Søn blev som Menneske født,
Og dog af sin Samtid miskendt og forstødt;
Den vilde ej tro paa en Menneske-Gud,
Og derfor med Haan de ham kastede ud.

Og dog var den Sandhed han bragte saa klar:
at Mennesket skabt i Guds Billede var,
At Jesus selv kom fra vort himmelske Hjem
Og Menneskets Slægtskab til Gud satte frem,
At ikke blot Fader men Moder var der
Tillige med Aandernes talrige Hær.

Da, eftersom Skyerne skifte og fly,
og danne paa Himlen den herligste By,
Jeg syntes at kende mit himmelske Hjem,
Og henrykt jeg søgte at trænge mig frem;
Men da, i det samme, jeg hører de Ord:
„Din Gerning er ikke tilende paa Jord!"

[1909]

A Heavenly Vision

(TRANSLATED BY MARTIN PULIDO)

When the Sun set and spread its glowing sheet
Of gold upon fields, flowers, and trees—
Upon mountaintops and overflowing the edges of clouds,
That gilded glimmer rebounding off the glass of lakes,
Then I saw through the veil a glimpse of Home,
And thoughts of Heaven drew me upwards.

I found myself in Heaven with God
And heard him issue the almighty decree:
"Let there be light!"—And out of Chaos, World sprang.
As God set in motion each thing in order,
I seemed to hear the Sons of God singing together
And shouting for joy over newly made Earth.

A dwelling place for the human family prepared—
And Adam as the chosen Forebearer,
The first of all, the eldest on Earth,
"The Ancient of Days" according to God's Word,
Of God's family and a heavenly prince
He was and will remain our family patriarch.

And the woman—a Daughter of Eve
Was the Savior's Mother on this sphere.
The Son of the Highest was born among men,
And yet rejected and misunderstood by his own.
They would not believe in a human God,
And therefore cast him out.

And yet the truth he brought was clear:
That humans were created in the image of Gods
That Jesus himself came from our heavenly Home
And man's relationship to deity he set forth,
That not only Father but Mother was there
Amongst the numberless heavenly hosts.

Then as the clouds shifted and flew,
And shaped in the sky the most glorious City,
I seemed to recognize my heavenly Home;
And overjoyed I sought to enter;
But in that moment, I heard these words:
"Your work is not finished on Earth!"

[2016]

To My Fellow Workers

Comrades, listen to my story,
Listen to the song I sing;
We must fight the battle bravely,
We must soar on eagle wing.

While the Morning stars were singing,
Ere the earth received its birth,
We were chosen by the masters,
Now we live to prove our worth.

Father, Mother, blessed us yonder,
When we lived in realms of light,
There we vowed to live for others,
Here we stand for truth and right.

Yet we do not all remember,
What we did on yonder shore,
But our faithful silent teacher,
Will reveal the light once more.

Deeply hid within our being,
Is the record of the past,
When we learn to love and listen,
It will give us all we ask.

Let the stars sing on forever,
Let the living waters flow,
Let the angry tempests darken,
Let our hearts with kindness glow.

Hear the music in the distance—
Father's summons, mother's song;
"Come our children, we are waiting,
Join again our happy throng."

What a moment, we are coming,
Coming home with songs of cheer.
Father, Mother, we are coming
When we see our pathway clear.

Comrades, let us stand united,
While our hearts beat warm and true.
We must work a moment longer,
Ere we wing our flight anew.

[1910]

PART TWO

On the Far Shore

1973 – 2003

CAROL LYNN PEARSON

The Family of Light

Kindled into the family
That sparked the sun
We came—
With suns and moons and stars
In us forever.

And the Mother
Who nurtures new light
In the warmest of all wombs,
And the Father
Who holds in His hands
The growing glow and blows it brighter—
Together placed us in another room.

It is dark here.
Deep within element
We dim and dim.
And to slim the ray
That might find its way out
We handcraft clever bushels
Of modest, fashionable fears.

But long darkness is untenable
And we yearn for the burning
To begin again.

We have had too much night.
Shall we—
Shall we together shed our bushels
And stand revealed—
Sons and daughters of light?

[1973]

Blessing

Spirit hands are on my head—
Father, Mother blessing me.
Comfort courses down like rain
Cleansing and caressing me.

[1983]

Parent Friends

There will come a time
When these little ones
That come to me now
For bandaids and sandwiches
Will not need a mother much.
Already they are done with my womb
And done with my breast.

They will always need the rest
Of me, I believe—arms, heart, mind.
But someday I expect to find
That we walk with matching stride
And talk of things
That friends talk of.

Will there come a time,
Sometime after time is done,
Sometime when I no longer come to you,
Dear Father and Mother,
For bandaids and sandwiches,
Will there come a time
When we walk with matching stride
And speak our common, godly concerns?

Sometime, when this infancy ends,
Can we be
Not only parent and child,
But friends?

[1983]

Within

I read a map once
Saying the Kingdom of God
Was within me
But I never trusted
Such unlikely ground.

I went out.
I scoured schools
And libraries
And chapels and temples
And other people's eyes
And the skies and the rocks,
And I found treasure
From the kingdom's treasury
But not the kingdom.

Finally
I came in quiet
For a rest
And turned on the light.

And there
Just like a surprise party
Was all the smiling royalty,
King, Queen, court.

People have been
Locked up for less, I know.
But I tell you
Something marvelous
Is bordered by this skin:

I am a castle
And the kingdom of God
Is within.

[1983]

In Celebration of the First Menstruation

Katy,
Who has of late been putting
Pads and panties
On her Keeshond dog
Briget Baby Brown Eyes,
Loped long-legged and twelve and sweet
Into my room today and giggled,
"Mom, Mom, I'm in heat!
I just started!"

I pulled her down
Into the big chair that we
Used to not quite fill
And made sure she understood
That a menstruating women
Is of the devil
That she must not
Look at the sun, sit in water
Speak to a man
For she is unclean
Or enter a church
For she would defile it.

And I stroked her
Innocent freckled skin
And bright braided hair
And told her to keep in mind
That she is, as St. Jerome said,
Formed of foul slime.
Katy laughed. "Right, Mom!"

And I told her all that was from
A bad period
Men's period
When male was god and jealous
And said what was what
A period that luckily menopaused.

But that there was an earlier time
When woman's secret was sacred
When the Great Goddess
Gave the blood of life
And all worshipped joyously
At her royal fountain
When girls "bore the flower"
A flower that flows a future fruit
Making her a marvel
A time that is due again.

Then I gave Katy five and said,
"Hey, woman, let's go celebrate!"
And we went right out under the sun
And Katy spoke right up to the man
And ordered a BLT and we ate.

We clicked our cups to flowering
And Katy giggled and blushed and bounced
And blessed the restaurant
With her presence.

[1992]

A Motherless House

I live in a Motherless house
A broken home.
How it happened I cannot learn.

When I had words enough to ask
"Where is my Mother?"
No one seemed to know
And no one thought it strange
That no one else knew either.

I live in a Motherless house.
They are good to me here
But I find that no kindly
Patriarchal care eases the pain.

I yearn for the day
Someone will look at me and say
"You certainly do look like your Mother."

I walk the rooms
Search the closets
Look for something that might
Have belonged to her—
A letter, a dress, a chair.
Would she not have left a note?

I close my eyes
And work to bring back her touch, her face.
Surely there must have been
A Motherly embrace
I can call back for comfort.
I live in a Motherless house,
Motherless and without a trace.

Who could have done this?
Who would tear an unweaned infant
From its Mother's arms
And clear the place of every souvenir?

I live in a Motherless house.
I lie awake and listen always for the word
That never comes, but might.
I bury my face
In something soft as a breast.

I am a child—
Crying for my Mother in the night.

[1992]

Support Group

You can fall here.
We are a quilt set to catch you
A quilt of women's hands
Threaded by pain made useful.

With generations of comfort-making
Behind us, we offer this gift
Warm as grandma's feather bed
Sweet as the Heavenly Mother's
Lullaby song.

You can fall here.
Women's hands are strong.

[1992]

Truth Eternal

"Thou shalt remain, in midst of other woe …
'Beauty is truth, truth beauty,—that is all'"
—John Keats, "Ode on a Grecian Urn" (1820)

There is beauty in that which has been,
never to be the same again;
when all outward evidence is gone,
the truth of that beauty lives on.

There is light in the dark before day,
as we strain to see its first faint rays;
in the absence of presence lingers a hope,
a fixed faith in the latent unknown.

There is truth in forgotten, unseen
life, it persists from the past like a dream,
in the memory of mothers and daughters of light
lives an endless divine archetype.

[1976]

(Written after hearing Carol Lynn Pearson speak about Daughters of Light)

Medusa's Prayer

Our Mother in Heaven is hidden,
fear hushed Her hallowed name;
no Queen to come,
Her will undone on earth
has shut Her in the heavens,
has given us Medusa
by rumor spread, to daily tread
where few will dare trespass
this trespass against us.
Leave us not, but let us tempt Her out,
and deliver Her from evil,
for She is Medusa in the kingdom
of the power and the glory of men,
forever.

[1990]

The Oracle at Nephi

I dreamed the aged Matriarch inside the Salt Lake Temple
was a youthful Medusae (nee Melissae), sequestered in a sealing
room with mirrors fully muralled in scenes of Eden.

This Medusa wrote a letter asking me to send a picture—
"So I can see you better," she pled. "They won't let me
have a mirror and it's lonely in This Place."

I looked, but couldn't find one good enough to send a
Gorgon. So I framed a passage from a page of my first book
and mailed it first class, with some postage due.

The image slowly faded to a dull and grey symposium in a
large and spacious building. I didn't stay, but started walking
in the dust, a dirt road to the desert, into an ancient time,
draped in white linen raiment drifting with my stride.

A sojourn from the city of Saints gave me strength.
I found my will, and made my way to the Oracle at Nephi,
a Sibyl of SanPete, shrouded in the south, hidden—
across the hill from Manti temple, to keep Her mantle pure.

"Are you a prophetess?" she tested, wresting a confession
with a riddle; the only real response was verse and rhyme.
Answers rising artesian, like fountains on Mount Olympus,
issued from a source as deep as taboo truth.

"Medusa was true and faithful, until she yearned to converse
with Perseus, unveiled; but Perseus was armed and dangerous,
ordained by Zeus and Moses. She appealed to her Sisters for
sororal aid, without avail. Alas, in fear and dread, Medusa
fled and hid herself, the Oracle at Lehi Roller Mills."

The Oracle at Nephi was silent in the face of Medusa mythos
and news of an Oracle at Lehi. She let me enter the Nephi temple
veiled in mystery of initiation, reunion, and integration of Self,
mending the rending of Adam-Eve (and naming Nephi's wife).

Erstwhile in Salt Lake sanctuary, Eve waited patiently for further
word from Mother ... but Medusa, who escaped the sealing room
by divining her way to Lehi, had discovered the sealed portion
of the golden plates, and located Lehi's lost pages.

I didn't see Her postscript at first glance, but here it is:
"P.S. Isis and Inanna invite you and the Fates to dinner.
Asherah and Hathor have appetizers, Melissa and Asenath
are serving dessert. Sophia and Diana say hello."

[1994]

(Dream after excommunication for an anthology of feminist theology)

First Grief

Last night, my daughter—
Mine by right of love and law,
But not by birth—
Cried for her "other mother."

Accountable
And duly baptized she may be,
But eight is young
For grown-up grief,
The first I cannot mend
With Band-Aids,
Easy words,
Or promises.

I cannot tell her yet
How I have also cried
Sometimes at night
To one whose memory
My birth erased;
Who let me go
To other parents
Who could train and shape the soul
She had prepared,
Then hid her face from me.

[1978]

Song of Creation

Who made the world, my child?
    Father made the rain
    silver and forever.
        Mother's hand
drew riverbeds and hollowed seas,
drew riverbeds and hollowed seas
    to bring the rain home.

Father bridled winds, my child,
    to keep the world new.
        Mother clashed
fire free from stones
and breathed it strong and dancing,
and breathed it strong and dancing
    the color of her hair.

He armed the thunderclouds
    rolled out of heaven;
        Her fingers flickered
            hummingbirds
weaving the delicate white snow,
weaving the delicate white snow
    a waterfall of flowers.

And if you live long, my child,
    you'll see snow burst
        from thunderclouds
    and lightning in the snow;
listen to Mother and Father laughing,
listen to Mother and Father laughing
    behind the locked door.

[1979]

U latti dâ matri

U latti dâ matri
nasci dô focu dô cori
e fa d'amuri suli lucenti.

Tannu n'agghiornanu matini
frischi comu i rosi
ntê manu di picciriddi.

E ni ncuntramu, nudi,
ammenzu l'àrvuli,
e nenti si po mmucciari.

U latti dâ matri
è furmatu ntê stiddi,
e nesci câ luci d'arba.

Attraversu 'a notti viaggia
sina c'arriva nterra,
e s'arrimina ntô pettu.

The Milk of the Mother

(TRANSLATED FROM THE SICILIAN)

The milk of the mother
is born from the heart's fire
and makes of love a brilliant sun.

Then, for us, mornings come
fresh as roses
in children's hands.

And we meet, naked,
among the trees,
and there can be no secrets.

The milk of the mother
is distilled in the stars
and pours with the light of dawn.

Across the night voyaging
until it reaches earth,
and there stirs in the breast.

[1980]

Another Prayer

Why are you silent, Mother? How can I
Become a goddess when the patterns here
Are those of gods? I struggle, and I try
To mold my womanself to something near
Their goodness. I need you, who gave me birth
In your own image, to reveal your ways:
A rich example of thy daughters' worth;
Pillar of Womanhood to guide our days;
Fire of power and grace to guide my night
When I am lost.
My brothers question me,
And wonder why I seek this added light.
No one can answer all my pain but Thee,
Ordain me to my womanhood, and share
The light that Queens and Priestesses must bear.

[1980]

Let My Sisters Do for Me

If we must preserve our differences,
Then let my sisters do for me.
Let my sister tear my last resistance
From my mother's womb, let her
Cradle me and give me my name,
Let her baptize me and call me forth
To receive the Spirit, let her
Teach me of the world, let her
Ordain me to womanhood, let her
(She does wash, anoint and clothe)
Be my god beyond the veil, let her
Heal my sickness, hold my baby, be my friend.
Let her dig my grave, let her robe me,
Let her bless my empty bones.
If you will not have me for your sister,
Then let my sisters do for me,
And let me greet my Mother on the far shore.

[1980]

To Mother in Heaven

The flowers you left for me
I found and pinned them to
my hair upon my wedding
day. And under a mountain
in Africa was found
the diamond you buried. Of
the gold of South America
was pressed the band I wear.

I think of you often.

I walk along the beach
and do not find your footprints.
But the shards of sun
you sowed, I follow towards
the veiled horizon.

I drove once through Wyoming
and saw how you had matched
the sage and mustard flowers
pretty little violet
wilds. It was lovely.

Your letters haven't yet
been found and bound.
Whenever black seeds lie upon
white snow or flocks aflight
embroider dawn, I look
for your writing.

At pollinating time
last year, close by the honey-
suckle, I breathed the air
of your perfume and wondered
if you had come perhaps
and I had missed you.

I try to remember what you
look like. Some nights
through my
reflection in our high window
I see the stars and think
I see strung diamonds plaited
in your hair. I think
if I could look into
the sun, I would see your
picture.

I want to know your name.
I know it is lovelier than Mary
or Sarah or Eve. Can you
please whisper it to me?
What is your name?

[1981]

Mother

I.

Mother, our first.
Nurturer of our souls.
You may have seen the world
as functional but plain.
So as a mortal
might bend over her
stitching to devise the decoration
for a barren room
did you, to adorn
our earthly home design

> an oak leaf, golden-red
> in a blue autumn sky;
> the fragrant lilacs, airy sweet
> after a spring rain;
> black birds stark against
> the snow bleached horizon?

Do you sit now by your
heavenly window, wishing its warmth
to light the way for
children gone too long?
Is the table set, the feast prepared?
And when you hear us call across the veil
will you run to kiss our brows
and warm our wayworn hearts

in the love
of a Divine Mother's embrace?

II.

Or, perhaps
Not just designer, but
        architect as well.
        Co-creator, executrix
No minute taker, you.

Our Advocate
        in the realms above,
your arguments
must bedazzle
packaged as they would be
        in offers of hope
        and undemanding
        love.

Despite these eons of
        amnesia,
        and our failure to
        call home,
You will wait on us with
infinite affection
and astound us with
your queenly reminiscences
and tales of our premortal
        training at
        your knee.

[1986]

Divestiture

And about all those brethren:
when Willene investigated the Gospel, she caught
the bus in Arlington, made one change, rode
past embassies, and met in a marble building
where ushers dismissed the congregation, one
red velvet row at a time, and no babies cried.

The bishop was hush-hush in the FBI,
the stake president a multi-millionaire,
an apostle sat on the stand. Her mission
president became a General Authority,
and on the day the Chairman of the U. S.
Tariff Commission confirmed her, she was asked
to record patriarchal blessings for the man
who'd translated the Book of Mormon into Japanese
while heading that mission. And that day
she also met the man she'd marry before
the year's end. One day in the Salt Lake Temple
intertwined endowment and marriage as if ties
to God tied on to a man.

Only when her husband walked off, did she begin
the divestiture of so many men. Twenty years
of cutting vestigial ties before the Good News
that neither Father nor Son can be confined
by all those brethren. Before the Full News
that the Mother must wait till enough Saints
fall to their knees and sanctify themselves with right pleas.

[1987]

Stellar Evolution

He was her sun and she was his earth,
his light was her warmth, her body his compass;
spinning through space in the chill of its dark
each plotted a course through the fulness of chaos
aiming to keep them turned to each other,
wrestling mass from the gut of the night
from the ghosts that they were, full of only self-knowing,
and fought against gravity, moving to dance.

She moved as a goddess, and he as a god:
his fingers were daylight and played in her weather,
her hair was a rainfall ending his drought.
The warmth of his face fell on furrow and bud.
He covered her bareness, she clad him in flesh
and sounding abysses as whales of grace
dancing an old fugue, two-stepping on water,
tumbled through waltzes that spun the whole ballroom.

They were the one god, female and male,
calling the universe out of its freeze-down,
heating their stew from a broth of free radicals,
generating from the heat of their friction
the flash of a few microseconds, the big bang
one final compression, one last stroke, away:
they were the one god, their "let there be" light—
and deft as leviathan, certain as night.

[1989]

Mother of Us All

> ... a certain woman of the company lifted up her voice,
> and said unto him, Blessed is the womb that bare thee,
> and the paps which thou hast sucked.
> (Luke 11:27)
>
> But woe unto them that are with child,
> and to them that give suck,
> in those days.
> (Luke 21:23)
>
> For, behold, the days are coming,
> in the which they shall say,
> blessed are the barren,
> and the womb that never bare,
> And the paps which never gave suck.
> (Luke 23:29)

Where are the ears that first heard me draw breath,
when all of infinity listened for every child to squall?
Where are the eyes that laughed in a flood of joy,
seeing that, like each child, I was born unlike any other?
Where are the lips that sucked venom from my heel,
the tongue that spat it back at the *fer-de-lance*,
the teeth that broke the spine of the serpent's helix?

For I would praise the mother I have never seen.

The heart that pumped her blood, though it were light,
    across the resistance of my earliest skin
    to warm me, bringing the starter-of-fire in,
    where is it, the heart that sang through my first dreams?
The womb that sheltered me when every part was potential,
    that tent, where is it, that held me against the vacuum,
    that cradled me in the bowels of mercy, sheltered,
    sanctioned the cleaving of sperm to egg, and called
    me from an infinitely distant point to the gravity well
    of her brilliant and massive charity—
    where is it, the womb that sheltered, the belly that bore me?
Where are the arms that cradled me at the breast,
    the hands that stroked my arms as I reached for the breast,
    the fingers that touched my cheek to open my mouth
    and guided the nipple into my opened mouth
    that I might feed upon the Milky Way,
    the wrist that curved the cupped hand round my heels
    that in my kicking I not dislodge the stars?

For I would praise the mother who will not die.

The buttocks that carried us upright against gravity,
    the thighs that kicked across the sea of stars,
    the feet that walked across the sands of Kolob
    where she held me, knees flexed against the gale,
    into the wind of that springtime world, to fly
    away, more like a seed than a hummingbird—
    where are the heels that bore the weight of my leaving?

When you wept to fill the oceans of this world
was I not there, although you wept for me?
When you sang the other beasts from slime to being
did I not shout for joy at their capering?
Was I already past the veil when last you kissed me
and whispered "Come home" when I could not hear,
but only feel your breath caress my cheek
which burns as if betrayed by recurved thorn?

Where is the fractured fading echo of your lament—
"For if they do these things in a green tree, what shall be done in the
dry?"
in a green tree
for if they do
for if they
in a green tree
they do these things
these things in a green tree
in a green tree,
do these things
they do
for if they do
in a green tree
these things in a green tree
they do
they do
in a green tree
what shall be done in the dry?

[1999]

A Psalm

At Heaven's throne, I cry for wisdom.
O Father, give me your instructions,
    O Mother, teach me of your laws.
    Let me know You, that I may know myself.
    If you are silent, then I am bereft.
    Have I denied you, Mother, unaware?
    Have you stretched out your hand, and I not seen?
    Have you cried vainly at the gates, and I not heard?
    Or have I heard, and yet not known your voice?
    O Mother, give me your instructions,
O Father, teach me of your laws:
that I may follow, whole of heart.

[1989]

Our Mother Who Is With Us

Which of you mothers,
If your child cries out in the night,
Will not hear her cries,
And go to her,
And put your arms around her,
And comfort her?
If you, then, being weak,
Know how to comfort your children,
How much more does our Mother in Heaven
Comfort us when we stand in need of comfort?

Or which of you mothers,
If your child is confused
Or has a problem
Will not give him counsel?
If you, then, lacking knowledge of the future,
Know how to counsel your children,
How much more does our Heavenly Mother
Guide us when we ask to know what we should do?

Or which of you mothers,
If your child asks you a question,
Will send him away?
If you, then, being ignorant of many things,
Know how to enlighten your children,
How much more does our Mother in Heaven
Give truth to those who seek it?

Or which of you mothers
Does not know that your children
Need you to be with them?
If you, then, being selfish,
Will sacrifice to be with your children,
How much more is our Mother, not in heaven,
But here with us?

[1991]

To Our Mother in Exile

Before I was born
You were the One
In whom I lived
And moved
And had my being.

When I took my first breath,
You were there,
And put me to your breast,
And filled me up.

When I awoke alone,
Engulfed by darkness,
And cried out,
It must have been your arms
That picked me up
And held me close.

It must have been your finger
On the page of my first book,
Pointing to the pictures,
Your chin upon my head,
And your voice
Teaching me the names.

But somewhere, Mother,
In my going forth into the world,
Sometime, Mother,
In my growing,
And discovering,
And achieving,
And making a place
For myself in the world,
I didn't need you
And you disappeared.

I took care of myself,
Earned my own way,
Bought and sold,
Obeyed the Law,
And worshipped the Lawgiver.

But now I am a mother myself.
My body is used,
Used up.
Alone with my child,
I am engulfed with wonder
And I awake
To the arrogance of my march.
The mystery in my baby's eyes
Undoes me,
And the gentle tug at my breast
Draws me to you.

I want to know you, Mother.
I want to see your face.

[1996]

The Father and the Mother

Come let us praise The Father and The Mother
whose voices wrap around us in the night
whose arms enclose the darkest places of our hearts
whose tears ran on the mountains of Gettysburg and Seoul,
of Sodom and Chernobyl.
They are weeping for their children they are weeping love
small lures falling, waiting to be taken,
to be tangled in the piece of sun
given to their children
waiting for the cleansing fire to light the earth,
making it plain as the love by which we were conceived.

[1991]

God's Muse

In Heaven there is a slender woman
who smiles a lot. This is her job and
she does it well. Her boss is God but
she calls him "that old leviathan"
and snickers at his clothing while he
pretends not to notice that he's never
been graced with her good favor or even
her genuine interest.

Some art fits in envelopes and perhaps
that is the best kind, personal and
immediate and sure of its audience
and no one in the world need lament
its demise: there's nothing glamorous
about the odd pitch of paper ripping
before it's cast in the trash,
nothing glamorous about some undertaker
in Egypt stuffing Sappho's shredded poems
into the mouth of a mummified crocodile.
Which is how the slender woman wants it.

Every day in the afternoon she practices
levitation for an hour. It's easy and
it bores her but it's the only time
no one dares bother her and in those
sixty precious minutes she designs
monuments to the powers denied her.
All things small, intricate and dangerous,
all spiders and poisons and viruses,
those are the handiwork of God.
Whales and mountains and oceans,
all things spacious and sublime,
are the dreams of the bored slender woman.
It's God's job to fill them up.
He does it as well as he can.

[1992]

Souviens-toi, mon enfant

Souviens-toi, mon enfant: Tes parents divins
te serraient dans leurs bras, ce temps n'est pas loin.
Aujourd'hui, tu es là, présent merveilleux,
ton regard brille encore du reflet des cieux.
Parle-moi, mon enfant, de ces lieux bénis
car pour toi est léger le voile d'oubli.

Souviens-toi, mon enfant des bois, des cités.
Pouvons-nous ici-bas les imaginer?
Et le ciel jusqu'au soir, est-il rose ou gris ?
Le soleil attend-il la neige ou la pluie?
Conte-moi, mon enfant, la couleur des prés
et le chant des oiseaux d'un monde oublié.

Souviens-toi, mon enfant: A l'aube des temps,
nous étions des amis jouant dans le vent.
Puis un jour, dans la joie nous avons choisi
d'accepter du Seigneur le grand plan de vie.
Ce soir-là, mon enfant, nous avons promis
par l'amour, par la foi, d'être réunis.

[1993]

O Remember, Little One

(TRANSLATED BY MARTIN PULIDO)

O remember, little one, your Parents Divine
held you close in their arms, not long ere this time.
Now today you are here: marvelous, alive,
and your eyes still reflect heaven's brightest light.
Tell me now, little one, of that blessed place,
for you make light the veil that locks mem'ry's gates.

O remember, little one, heaven's towns and groves?
Here below, do you think we can picture those?
Is the sky pink or gray at the close of day?
Is a sun, warm and fair, cloaked by snow or rain?
Tell me now, little one, colors of their plains.
Sing me bright songs of birds from worlds far away.

O remember, little one, at the dawn of days
we were there, best of friends, in the wind we'd play.
Then one day, we felt joy, when this choice arrived:
to accept, from the Lord, the great plan of life.
That evening, little one, firmly we agreed
by our love, by our faith, that once more we'd meet.

[2013]

She Who Has No Name

charms snakes;
listens late to country radio;
knits a sky white-full of stars;

rides up front in buses;
jumps bad double dutch;
cleans nobody's house but her own;

reaches for that second helping;
Sunday mornings dances salsa;
hikes Timp to name her wildflowers;

takes pot brownies to AIDS patients;
pats masa on her hands;
sang back-up for Etta James, Lady Day;

stops to fix your flat at night
in her red 64 Chevy pickup—
rounded fenders, no gun rack;

carries picket signs and aspirin;
tells a campfire tale so wild
it melts the sap off the pines;

laughs head-back-heart-pounding;
strings a mean cats' cradle;
wears turquoise, cowries, clover chains;

no push-up bra, no platform shoes
(to please anyone but her lovely self);
kneads raw earth with her knuckles;

scores the winning goal
(half of Latin America screams!);
has a good husband who minds His own business;

says, "I'm glad you came all this way;"
says, "don't you mess," and means it;
says, "girl, treat yourself right."

You listen. She looks just like you re-membered her.

[1995]

Adam-Ondi-Ahman (Excerpt)

Adam-Ondi-Ahman tells the story of Adam and Eve's journey around the world to summon their children to a grand family council, accompanied by a very young Methuselah, scarcely a hundred years old. In this scene they have been telling him what happened in Eden and why they left.

~

"One day," Eve said, "when Adam came in from the fields, we sat and stared at each other for a long time, and finally said, 'How did Satan know?' We called on the name of our Father many days to understand this thing, for it troubled us greatly. After many days—I want you to understand how unusual this was— Father and Mother both came (this was very unusual) and stood before us.

There was silence for a space, until we asked, 'You knew the serpent was listening. Why did you speak to him through us? Why could you not keep him out of the Garden?'

After a time, Father spoke,

'There was in the land of Uz a man named Job.
Whole he was and upright he stood before the Lord.
Until Satan one day stood before the Lord.
Had you given me all you have given Job, would not I,
    even I, honor you?
Let me reach my hand out and take it, and Job will stand
    before you and curse you.'

And Satan did. But Job blessed the name of the Lord.

And Satan stood before the Lord and said,
'Behold the family of Job.
Would not I, even I, bless you had you given me such
    a family as Job's?
Would not I, even I, honor you?
Let me reach out my hand and take it, and Job will stand
    before you and curse you.'

And Satan did. And Job knelt before the Lord and blessed the
    memory of his children and the name of his Lord.

And Satan stood before the Lord and laughed at
    prostrate Job and said,
'Behold the skin of Job.
How comforting it is, all tanned and wise with age.
No ticks.
Nothing to itch.
It holds his bones in, but does not bind them, swelling the joints.
Would not I, even I, bless you had you given me such
    supple skin as Job's?
Let me reach my hand out and take the comfort,
    and give instead boils,
And Job will stand before you and curse you.'

And Satan did. And Job sat down in ashes, and took
   a broken pot and scraped himself,
And his dog licked Job's wounds.
And Job's wife said, 'Curse God and die.'
But Job said, 'Were the All-loving to stand before me
He would smooth my skin, wipe my tears, wash my ashes.'"

Eve stood. "Oh, that the All-loving would stand before me. That's
   what he said. But I must rest."

"Well, did He?" Methuselah said.

"Certainly. And a most wondrous vision. Have you ever seen great
   whales? When we get to the ocean perhaps."

"Continue the story please," Methuselah said.

"Another time," Eve said.

"But He didn't answer the question. He didn't say why he let Satan
   overhear. Or, you haven't gotten that far?"

"Well, he never quite said. Didn't need to. You see, we understood
   he was talking about himself."

"Well, yes, of course. It begins with Satan standing before God,"
   Methuselah said.

"No, no," Eve said. "When Father finished speaking, I turned to my
   Mother and asked her, 'Did you really tell him to curse God and
   die?' 'Yes I did,' she answered. 'Oh yes. Indeed I did. Yes.'"

[1997]

strange gods

i lust after strange gods
the god who blesses the black sheep
in the hardwood pews of a despised denomination
the woman who lays her dark head on the shoulder
of an even darker woman, and sings
"faith of our fathers," leaning into the hymn even
as she leans into her lover's embrace

the god who blesses the woolly head of the old ram
wise ram crowned with an unruly shock of white
stopped making the music of the herd
when it ceased to fill him with ecstasy
but is still charged with the static
electricity of the mountaintop
bless the lambs who see the lightning in his eyes

i lust for the god of black gospel
who deposits us in calvary's dark vestibule
then opens the door to the light where the choir
sings "i'll fly away," and mahogany women in white
gloves usher us into a heaven where the reverend
gary davis, sonny terry, brownie mcghee, queen ida,
skip james and odetta shake the walls with their voices

i lust for the veiled god
who will not go to war with her children
will not author famine or floods
will not prune the buds of her most promising flowers
in some grand apocalypse
will reveal her face at the wedding with the bridegroom
i lust after strange gods

[1997]

God Plans Her Day

7:00   Shower for an hour in monsoon off Manila.

8:15   Name the falls in Tanzania.

9:00   Get the New World Feminist edition of the Koran.

9:45   Plan the unveiling for a Friday afternoon.

11:00   Repair the tear in the firmament.

12:30   Eat something. Sip the milk of human kindness.

1:45   Get my O-rings checked. Arrange for more ozone.

2:45   Tender my regrets to Chicken Tenders on proposed
         endorsement deal.

3:15   Nap in the Lap of the Gods.

4:00   Play with the kids.

5:15   Hike to Mt. Baldy.

6:15   Picnic in the wild (Baked Alaska).

7:15   Resist the temptation to relocate.

7:30   Listen to my scratchy old 33⅓ of Judy Roderick.

8:30   Pray for rain in the Oklahoma Panhandle.

9:00   Blank verse.

10:15   Read in bed.

10:45   Spank the pillow.

[2003]

Motherless Child

Do we grieve the missing wildness of the Mother?
Patriarchs and theologians may not bother

to detect her incandescence in their dreams.
But on reflection, may we come to recognize

her image in the sea or see the way her shadow plays
the craters of the moon? How soon might science bare

her essence in our DNA or find her tangled in the blood
of tigers on the banks of the Zambezi stream?

When something just outside my memory refracts
a glimmer of her glory, I want to ask, whose child am I?

In the equation of creation, why was she expunged
and, and in the book of history, her chapters purged?

I glimpse a future when I may read the body
of her work and see the vistas of her soul unfurled.

Pending that dawn, sometimes I feel she's almost gone.

[2003]

On the Mountain Road to Taos

Outside of Santa Fe, high above our road,
    an out-of-place Van Gogh sky rapts us in,
    swirls and hovers, blue shading pale to navy.

This sky is southwest, America big, takes up all
    the space it can, weighs on the horizon,
    presses down on stones, subdues the mountain
    and mesa fringe.

At the height of the hills, cedars yield naturally to tall pines,
    saw-jagged and sharp on the ridges, coyote's teeth,
    irritating the soft underbelly of the Western sky.

Never mind. The blue seems to jiggle with laughter
    as we move along the mountain road to Taos.

Cotton puff-ball clouds, gray beneath, billowy white above,
    scud indolently across the deep sky, prompt us toward
    a child's wish to fall from airplanes, trample a bit
    on a pillowed bed as we did at Wildwood.

Due north, as we run, candy-like rock mountains,
    resist the push of the sky, hoist themselves into view.

Maynard, Dixon that is, would have loved to get
  a paintbrush on these. Maybe he did. Not that they
  need much touching up, nature did it pretty well
  first time around.

And Georgia did it better than anyone else, nearly better
  than God herself. Georgia painted them stark,
  and clean, with colors not in nature.

She painted them plain, and complex, then plain again—
  made these mountains and mesas hers, then ours,
  then put them back here for us to see.

[1998]

Missing God

I don't remember
her voice.

But sometimes
in the mountains
I think I hear
an echo

of the flute
she played.

[1998]

PART THREE

A Fearsome Beauty

2007 – 2017

ALEX CALDIERO

How She Goes

How she goes & dips into the living dictionary & one by one or two by three pulls out the words & places them gently, naturally onto the page in a new-found order that would express & tell what she wants to share by the sheer act of her will & grace commune & communicate such feelings & thoughts that enlarge the sensibility of her audience and press their ears up to heaven's walls so they become ear witnesses to what she so poignantly utters & places upon that side of the scale which needs to tip during the measuring and weighing of the human heart and render it (the heart) lighter than a feather against all her words and deeds and thereby save this soul by sheer beauty and make it soar free by the powers of poetry reach the boundaries where the mind turns into a feral creature of light and the heart is indistinguishable from its thoughts borne on winged steeds to new heights of eloquence past metaphor & time singing, oh how she draws it out of me & I readily give in: daughter of the muses, midwife.

[2007–08]

Once Upon a Time

Once upon a time the beautiful lady asked
"Is this poetry?"

She let her self sit for a moment and smiled.
There was no longer any reason to fear an
answer, so she asked again: "Is this poetry?"

It was right after the time had elapsed in which
the absence of the king had passed without any one
noticing neither the time nor the king. It was a mythic
moment in the lives of humans who were just
beginning to start to wonder who and how they had
come upon the notion of themselves.

Without reason, her mouth began to speak a
poem word by word until the last word was
about to be almost too much to bear.

"Is this poetry?" she asked and sat back and
let herself be looked at closely—her skin
was soft to the eye; her breath hot to the eye;
her clothing invisible to the eye—eyes only could
fathom the depth of her body's weight
upon the chair same as upon and against
the body of the beholder whose eyes
mean something wonderful is happening.

"Les diamants," she said without moving her lips.
"My songs are such poor witnesses," she added and
let herself be looked at even closer.

The texture of her skin was in-credible, even as
the eyes got their fill and should have closed
but instead kept coming closer to enjoy
microscopic details of pure delight.

The ideal mattress should not be as soft
nor as inviting as her arms, and yet to
sleep was the only thought that had
not found its way back home.

"Put your hands on my eyes," she said to the very
eyes that had wanted to take
her in and into themselves find the meaning
of who she really was.

Poetry could start at any moment—it did.
There was no longer any reason to ask or to wonder.

[2007–08]

Excerpt from "Quantum Gospel: A Mormon Testimony"

1

Symmetry exists in exact reflections of Love:
Take a patch of chaos circling beforehand,
Sling it past black stars circling at random,
Create light in rings inside particled sparks,
Glowing in random points and recognitions,
Moving and brewing beneath your own hand.
Respond to Word of God inside your mind:
Call the involvement creation, as the eyes
Of the Gods gaze infinity into finite forms.

2

Had I reckoned further I would have wakened
A dream of being being born inside my mind;
Had I known my urging soul, inviting my eyes,
To behold myself admitting a verge of sky,
Had I been born a babe unto regenerations,
Electric with crackling insights and intuitions,
I would have borne witness to the Holy Soul,
Whipping like lightning the spark embedded,
The rumbling inside, my own seething Vortex.

3

Where did I begin, beside the counsels of God?
The intelligences swarming like flaming bees
About the instigations of the centered glory,
Unfettered, as multicolored gardens explode
In waves of flowers, streaming beaming leaves,
Vanguards of redeeming Impulse, to be living,
The very air alive with incessant buzz of Love,
The desire for good and sheer deep believing,
Redoubted in swarms, informed by beauty alone.

4

Heaven gleaned as home, taken as a given form
Of loving, Father and Mother, intent on feeding
The baby beam, redeemed from an infinite river
Of flashes, flowing by the garden of belonging,
The place of becoming, the seed of my being,
Where I began, uninformed and searching, to see,
My harvest of options returning upward to the sun,
Redeemed, to become one with a hovering spirit:
The beginning of all beginnings, my beginning.

[2007]

Creation

The sun's ten fingers came unfurled.
He gathered struts and made a world.
With careful breath the sphere was blown:
a hollow ball of molten stone.
And with the glass-sharp stars in thrall,
he spun the geodesic ball.

The moon stretched out her oyster hand
and on the struts she lifted land.
In mercury streams the valleys bled:
the mountain shook its hoary head.
She set the rain in silver sheets
upon the ocean's stormy streets.

The sun shook out his golden beard
and with its heat the land was seared.
The gold-gray ash, 'neath greening rain,
bristled up in heads of grain.
The trees grew up at his approach,
and closed their gowns with emerald brooch.

The moon unbound her swelling womb
and scattered the world with ruby bloom.
She shrouded its eyes with birds in flight
and veiled its face with silky night.
Then balanced the sphere on a silver scale
and lined the seas with fishes' mail.

Then the sun and the moon
set the world in a swoon
and clothed it in meadow and wood.

And with bashful glance
began to dance

... and called it good.

[2009]

Invocation / Benediction

Father, Mother, help me piece together the contradictions of my
    life:
White cotton, red satin, brown polka dot; torn Sunday dress,
    Navajo rug, frayed baby blanket.
Make me insistent on every lonely shred, willing to sacrifice no one.
Where there is no pattern, God, give me courage to organize a
    fearsome beauty.
Where there is unraveling, let me draw broad blanket stitches of
    sturdy blue yarn.
Mother, Father, give me vision.
Give me strength to work hours past my daughters' bedtime.
Give me an incandescent all-night garage
with a quorum of thimble-thumbed grandmothers sitting on
    borrowed folding chairs.
We will gather all the lost scraps and stitch them together:
A quilt big enough to warm all our generations:
all the lost, found, rich, poor, good, bad, in, out, old, new, country,
    city, dusty, shiny ones;
A quilt big enough to cover all the alfalfa fields in the Great Basin.
Bigger. We are piecing together a quilt with no edges.
God, make me brave enough to love my people.
How wonderful it is to have a people to love.

[2010]

Names of God the Mother

The One	Our God Throughout All Times and in Eternity
Womb of Creation	The Everlasting Mother
Almighty God	The Great High Priestess
Watcher of the Watchers	Keeper of the Times
Mother God	God the Mother
Tree of Life	Root, Branch, and Leaf of the Tree
Eve	Mother of All Living
Mother Earth	Zion
Asherah	Bride of Christ
Wisdom	Sophia
The Holy Spirit	The Light of Truth
The Dove	Lady of Peace
The Comforter	Counselor
Sanctifier	Purifier
God with Us	God among Us
Zion Above	Zion Below
Wonderful	Marvelous Worker

The One Who Never Left Us But Is Lost	The One Who Never Left Us and Is Found
Seed of the One	Beloved Daughter
Earth Mover	Dragon Slayer
Ensign to the Nations	An Army with Banners
Blade of Freedom	Sword of Justice
The One Called from Everlasting...	...To Recall Us to Eternity

This poem is in chiastic form. The first column should be read down from the top and the second up from the bottom. The names read across are paired, giving a theology of the being, roles, and works of God the Mother.

[2011]

Message to Cecily

A great loneliness has now descended:
Within you there is a space that yearns,
A heart-hollow—to teach you to return
And to watch for Me, which I have intended.

From now on I shall leave messages for you.
You will see them everywhere you glance;
In the temple's spire and in the starry dance
When the evening sky turns that certain shade of blue.

I have not deserted you; I am near.
You will hear Me outside your window at morn,
You will hold Me when your daughter is born,
And kiss Me whenever you wipe away a tear.

Look for Me when your sorrow is deep as the sea:
I am the Mother whose touch is tender and light,
I am the Sister holding your hand at night,
I am the Lover who woos you back to Me.

[2011]

Where is Mother?

Mother has living blood,
veins blue and moving,
like Earth.
She speaks soft,
as loud as shining morning.
Her skin is one thousand roads
driven on dust and rock and grit.
We suck Her sighs into our breast,
a breeze, breathing this whisper
from Heaven.
She bleeds, She bleeds,
can you hear Her?

[2011]

Invocation

May the weary, sighing for God's embrace, feel themselves cradled
in her arms.

May those who desire to know their Mother and are not satisfied
with less know joy.

May those who give themselves away to know her dwell in
Wisdom's home.

May those who desire her coming, but cannot believe, be
comforted. God speaks through the honest.

May those who long for her presence, but have family and friends
who are troubled, feel her love.

May those who are troubled because of sisters or brothers who talk
with our Mother, but give them place, feel God's love.

May those who cannot find her in religion hear her voice in
contemplation, feel her caress in the wind, and see her likeness
in others.

May those who love truth and seek for justice, freedom, and light
find that they are Wisdom's disciples.

May those who pray for new eyes and ears discern her presence and
know that it could be her breath blowing love into their hearts
and vision into their minds.

May those who seek her in sacred books find her.

May those who seek see in Jesus' gracious words and works the acts
of the Daughter also.

May those who call out to Father in need be granted wisdom to
   discern when the Mother's voice answers.
May those who can accept God as woman see God's image in their
   own reflection.
May those who do her work be called her children and those who
   walk her paths meet her on the way.
May those whose words of desire—bursting from their lips—call for
   the veil to be lifted, see her revelation.

[2012]

Here the Whole Time

I was barely a teen when you appeared in my dreams
of chapels and sacraments; gentle, wise, wordless guide
offering holy water in crystal brimmed with light.
I thirsted for first communion with you at thirteen,
thwarted by those who stopped the wellspring.

You reappeared in glimpses, "a movement and a rest"
in my peripheral vision, a moment in a mirror, a flutter
in the breeze, you walked with me invisible, a presence
approaching or retreating, ever reticent.

Both of us were ghosts, unrecognized potentials
in my mind, grasping for a more solid sense of self.
I saw outlines, phantoms, shadows, not embodied
spark, incarnate light, intelligence, truth.

Yet, you were there all along, I recalled the night my soul
awoke inside a dream—you appeared within my Spirit.
"Who are you?" I asked. "You know me," you said.
"Sophia," I breathed ... Wisdom. World Soul. Paraclete.

You were there the whole time, animating life all around me,
in the eyes of every woman and man, in the songs of children,
cries of babes, in laughter and pain, the world was your witness,
the soul of every human being was your home.

You were here the whole time, between the words that tried
to say you were not here, could not be known—you were here
within texts that talked of trees and groves, of wisdom and vision,
in imagery and meaning, in missing lines of liturgy and history.

You were here, the whole time.

[2012]

My Turn on Earth

I sing in praise of the High God!
Material Father.
Embodied Mother.
He that sorrows and weeps.
She that worries and cries.
Praise Him!
Praise Her!
For they stood and said, "These!"
"Praise them, we also are these!"
"And these will be made like us!"

And lo.
And lo.

There was a place.
There was a space.
Where matter was not yet matter.
Unorganized.
Wandering.
Here and there ascatter.

(The Spell)

Knot it.
Bind it.
Fasten it with glue.

Hold it.
Twist it.
Into a matter stew.

Shrink it.
Crush it.
Until it's just a tittle.
Pack it.
Stack it.
Until it cannot wiggle.

Until … ?

Until Bang!
Until KaBoom!
Expanding space
Extending time

And then there was light.
And it all seemed quite right.

The children gathered round to watch
the great unfolding.

"Patience," said Father.
"Patience," said Mother.

And then a swirl soft lit appeared,
Of stars thick spinning through the cloud,
Then another and another graced the expanding mere,
As light through night serenely plowed,
Then for joy the sons cried at a universe made,
And in ecstasy daughters clapped and sang,

For the foundation of delight was in matter laid,
And from that beginning all that would later emerge sprang,
"How long?" his children begged and pled,
"Before our warm bodies completed stand?
What wait before complexity will widely spread,
That we may in doughy matter gently land?"
"No one knows," said God, "What the future holds,
But we must watch and wait until it all unfolds."

Great is Their wisdom!
Mighty is Their watching!
Praise His mighty patience and Her forbearance!
For the universe spins as it must spin,
with matter in motion,
the laws are set,
and waiting and patience,
are also Godly acts.
For not until consciousness enters the worlds,
can They be heard and Their hand be raised.
For moving matter from those
courses to which it has been set
requires mind,
and mind matter.
And every act an agent.
And for every agent an act.

But lo, what horror did wetness unfold!
For substance found swift ways to replicate,
And thus began generations untold,
For suffering—pain undergird the second estate,
For through blood, semen and terrors thick rife
Complexity crawled mad in to the universe,
Growing, adding, emerging quickening life,

Bringing blessings though in curses immerse,
Then wept daughters and cried the sons at sere
Earth's monstrous demands in blood and tooth,
"Is there no other way?" wept mouths tight in fear
And Father answered, "Will you know the truth?
If freedom complexity and creativity will reign,
Matter must face its existential bane."

Then star bringer held up his hand.
And God nodded.
Mother bid him rise.

Stand still sweet parents swift and bright
Holding back darkness, wielding light

For I have found the Apollonian way,
No need for messes, wet with clay

No blood, no semen, or menstrual mess
No offal, sickness, age, distress

Make it craftily designed and certain,
Forget this grassy, slimish, verdan'

Here's how ...

(And the children listened as he spake)

Tick tock tick tock
Turn the steel precision gear
Now wind up the iron clock

Metal to metal, key to lock
Torsion, tension, forces shear
Tick tock tick tock

I will teach you how to walk
Set courses given, never veer
Now wind up the iron clock

All is determined, never ad-hoc
All to metronome adhere
Tick tock tick tock

Set with pulley, tackle, block
Let all in lockstep-click appear
Now wind up the iron clock

Toward exact prediction flock!
And every outcome engineer!
Tick tock tick tock!
Now wind up the iron clock!

A lone figure walks in the distance, His head bowed,
As the machinist unfolds blueprints
Exact and precise and shows his devisings.

The figure kneels and wonders,

Is a less cruel way possible?
Can this cup be replaced?
Can complexity emerge from other than freedom,
variation, inheritance, selection?
Is the machinist right?
Or is there another way?

The contriver can be seen
waving his hands and building a scale model
of a universe engineered to be set, certain,
no slop, all is measured and precise,
fixed, so that no surprises enter in.

The machinist shouts, "Where all is arranged from the beginning.
And once in motion it starts to spin—
all ends are determined from
What beginning laid."

The other looks upward, is there hope in him?

While the Bringer with tinker toys played and stacked,
Another looked at heaven's ecologies,
At life manifold, diverse within spheres,
Turning, emerging, knots in knots folding,
Living things striving upward creative,
Evolving, ascending, to new rife forms.

Who would enter this chaos? Pinning forms,
Spirit and matter joined, new made and stacked
Together, forged by bold acts creative,
To enable celestial ecologies,
To embrace topological folding,
So severe as to rupture holy spheres?

Alone to deftly hold those spinning spheres
Crashing, in sins of many confounding forms?
Who would stand to embrace such bleak folding?
Such a cross to bear! Against the world stacked!
On whom the fate of all ecologies,
Would rest? Who can dare be so creative?

As to fashion salvation creative
And reckless, to transcend all mortal spheres?
To save meek creaturely ecologies,
And those of keen humans whose godly form
Strains among its temptations sharply stacked,
And who against nature's lien is folding?

Who will stand to face staid fate's unfolding?
Against dark evil's relentless creative
Disillusionment, fierce against us stacked?
Search high and low among heavenly spheres,
Hunt among all conscious, sentient forms,
For one to hold tight the ecologies,

Willingly, lovingly, ecologies
Thick wrapped with matter and spirit folding,
Able to embrace hallow living forms,
And perform an act, holy, creative,
Beyond that which as yet emerged in spheres,
Endlessly spinning or in fell worlds stacked.

Who made the ecologies creative?
I. Send me therefore folding into spheres,
Where I will free willing forms, saved well-stacked.

"No don't send him send me! Send me. Send me," ticked the Tock,

I can engineer this with certainty,
such that none will be lost.
For every gear will turn as turned,
and every piece in place,
completing the whole

with exactness,
well designed,
ably constructed,
fit to all existence's need.
And all outcomes sure.

And then the tick-tock man of morning light sang:

Brood on blood spilled in thick fetid fluids that drain,
in a broth of anguish lapped by tongues wet—
slick behind bone teeth made to tear, crush, set
within flesh made to feel every rush of pain.
Watch razor claws that leave wounds spelling bane—
not quick, nor merciful—a constant threat
that mad suffering will never abet—
leaving on existence naught but a stain.
That fate on creature, will thus fall to us,
and alone will our bleak children fall dashed,
smitten by nature's relentless cunning.
Think hard what cruel gains come of such a thrust,
where all we love can be cut and slashed—
leaving us from mortal fears ever running?

Father / Mother in answer wept,

Since in complexity is freedom,
and machines made, even of
sweet biology are still machines.
We chose He that chooses life
over overt design.
We chose flourishing over
mandated determinism.

And they chose the life-giver.

And the intelligent designer was angry and kept not his first estate.

And Mother and Father gathered their children around them and said:

A Trilobite of order Redlichiida,
Evolved into an Asaphida,
Though they all went extinct
Their time on Earth quite succinct
Permian seas still contained some Proetida.

Fish arrived in Devonian Oceans
With fins they could use for all their motions
For limbs, hands, and feet
Are for Godlings quite sweet
And allow them to apply crafty lotions.

Amphibians soon came upon lands
And in doing so formed little hands
They could hold onto walls
And make squeaky calls
Meeting all their terrestrial demands.

Reptiles next appeared on the scene
(Some shaded a glorious green)
The dinosaurs bold
Or so we are told
Also had quite a wonderful sheen.

A great calamity struck the lan',
And smashed into an alluvial fan,
The dinosaurs died,
'cross the world wide

Bringing joy to a small mammal clan.

There once was a Therapsid from Nantucket,
Who evolved into a thought bucket,
Finally stood on two feet,
And with spears hunted meat,
Using language all the better to thunk it.

Two alone stand and watch,
Hand in hand, waiting, wondering.

Could the machinist be right?
Could the way of the gear's precise turning,
engineered with care, laid out in set
exactitude without play—smooth running,
machines clicking and clacking forward
in righteousness, humming sweetly, into a
shiny and grinding future been
better in the end?
Many have followed him after all.

She turns to him,

> "They will worship him when they get below."
> "I know."
> "The designer God."
> "Yes."
> "Omnipotent."
> "Yes, working through consciousness has its limitations.
>   Much better the myth of the God who can engineer any
>   end."
> "Omniscient."

"Yes. In a deterministic world if you know the initial
   conditions all else follows. There is great comfort in
   such a system."
"Omnipresent."
Looking down and spreading his arms he answers, "And here
   I am that I am. An object. Made of matter like them."
She laughs, "Yes. Like them. Our children."
"They will build machines great and complex."
"It's what they do with them that matters."
"Yes."
"I wonder, will they care for the world? Will they know the
   time that went into that cactus? That flower? That
   snake, that bird in bright plumage a half billion years in
   the making? Will they treasure the emergence?"
"We shall see."

He looks across the expanse,

"Existence is hard."
"Yes."
"We must prepare them for it."
"Yes."
"We are not machines."
"No. But emergence has its pleasures."
"Yes."

Sperm, egg, wet cells, sticky fluids spilling, sloppy, silly things
slide across membranes inexact, error prone
accidents of selection slip, flesh swings,
through channels forming rough and brittle bone,
genes slip and slide through motions mostly right,
but cough and jerk from time to time, hiccup trip,

springs unwind, chemicals push through and fight,
splashing nonsense far and wide, loosing grip.
But from the grass the cheetah bolts, relentless.
Clear eyes focused on motion swift, fleeing.
Fleet legs stretching, back—a coiled spring, exactness.
Retractable claws in air stretch, seizing.
Chaos from below; quite a messy show,
but from above bides beauty's steadfast flow.

The children want the parents to hurry things along.
Evolution works at its own pace, selecting from
among the random variation, passing it on though
time, slowly. There are many false starts. Much waste.
The children become impatient.

Can you not by force move things forward?
Just a little stir of the pot?
To hurry things along a bit?
Must consciousness be the only influence?

Just a little stir of the pot,
would make the stirrer culpable, so
must consciousness be the only influence,
as matter in motion does what it will,

would make the stirrer culpable? So?
Bodies need to find joy,
as matter in motion does what it will,
with spirit to guide it to new ends.

Bodies need to find joy,
true, and claim those courses
with spirit to guide it to new ends.
But spirit needs a consciousness if it is to find expression

true, and claim those courses
shadowed by force and law.
For a spirit needs a consciousness to find its expression
in the courses through which matter flows

Shadowed by force and law,
constrain all, even I,
in the courses through which matter flows
from consciousness to consciousness.

Constrain all, even I,
so through soft influence I push,
from consciousness to consciousness,
my work to do,

so through soft influence I push
through you to put matter into motion,
my work to do,
only through you.

Through you to put matter into motion
all my glory, all my love is expressed.
Only through you
can the pot be stirred at all.

And so the children watched as things unfolded, emerged,
what wonders they beheld as things blossomed into being.

"Look, that Toodon goes upon two legs!
Its brain is large? Will it be our home?"

"Wait and see my children." Wait and see?
But no, a meteor strikes and all hope ends.

"But on that planet,
in that galaxy over there,
is that language?
On that one, hands?
On that far planet,
song like those in the heavens are sung?
There! There is an orb where intelligence reigns,
where behemoths use their trunks for tools,
then fashion more of rock and stone."

"Will that do? It's not like you in form, but it will do.
See they love and talk and sing like angels too?
Consciousness is there. Is it not? Can we go?"

"Patience my children, wait and see, perhaps for another,
but not for you."

"Then ... what's this? Little insectivores develop tiny hands,
their eyes are focused straight ahead.
We watch as selection does its work,
on variations, random
threads, passing down generations of
these tree dwellers
chattering free."

"Cross your fingers. Hold your breath."

"A promising beginning sure.
Sociality makes their brains to grow,
their repertoire of sounds
and gestures grow and mount."
 "Can it be so? They seem familiar."

Their tail grows smaller, the brain gets larger.

"Please, oh please. Let the tail go. Let it go!
Let it go away."

And it does. Down from the trees they come
and soon walking
develop a smooth and careful gait.
They hunt.
From rocks
they hammer tools.

One of the children cries:
"What a piece of work is protoman! How noble in reason!
how infinite in faculty! In form and moving how
express and admirable! In action how like an angel!
In apprehension how like a god!"

"Are they conscious
in just the right way?
Are the categories in place?
Can they reason, can they feel?
Can you touch their minds dear
God? Can you thus enter now
and influence the universe?"

And there, in Earth's glades,
a male and a female
human squat across from each other.
A gourd of red ocher in the male's hand,
each dip a finger,
into the bowl.
And each to each apply a stripe,
down the other's face.
A decoration.
And act of love,
making art.

And consciousness entered
into the world.

In just the right way.

[2012]

Mother

I am.
I exist.
Not somewhere.
Not in silence.
But there
in the hollows
of your heart,
in your veins
and blood and cells,
in your deepest memory,
I am there.

Neither rare nor
invisible, I am
everywhere
you look for me:
among great
mountains,
over vermillion
plains, under
cerulean seas,
in the smallest
flower, in a mustard
seed, in a tear
from your own eye.

Like rivers
I run to you
abundantly,
graciously.
Open your arms.
Take me.

Listen for my voice.
It speaks from the wind,
not the whirlwind,
from roses and lilies
not flaming trees,
from moons and stars,
supernova and suns.

I ride on the backs
of dolphins and unicorns.
I am the wings of doves,
the feathers of
superb lyrebirds,
the wild call of
ivory-billed woodpeckers,
songs of linnets and
long-legged thicketbirds.
I am a voice
not of warning but
of welcome—

Welcome to my garden where
without surprise
we will sit down
as before. Remember,
in me also you live
and move and have
your being—*my* being,
our being. Remember
you are.
We are.
I am.

[2012]

Her

For some reason
he kept wondering
what She looked like,
how She spoke,
how She carried
Herself.
He thought of his mother,
a raven-haired and porcelained
beauty.
Perhaps there was something
of her.
Then he remembered his wife,
dead now
but still alive
in his heart,
and surmised that at least some
of her
might reveal traces—
haloed hair,
blue eyes,
grace and generosity
without measure
and singing that echoed
heaven.
Next, he thought of his daughters,

bright and capable,
olive-skinned,
dignified, alive,
and his granddaughter,
whose imagination
could unweave the sun
to its smallest
reflection,
like stars in the
night sky.
Yes, he thought,
some of them was in
Her as well,
as was some of
Eve
and Mary
and also
Bathsheba
and the Magdalene.
Perhaps when She helped
shape the
first woman,
She encoded some of herself
in her hair,
in her eyes,
in her beautiful mouth
and rounded breasts,
planting seeds of Herself
deep down,
under her skin,
in her heart,

Heavenly Mother in Mormon Poetry

in dendritic cells
and genes,
so that
down the ages,
some trace of Her
survived
in every woman
on earth,
and watching them,
seeing them,
delighting in them,
even loving them,
was how he could
imagine Her.

[2014]

What will you call her?

compass of quantum foam
conduit of accommodation

juggler of change
absorber of dereliction

sacredly managed veil
of consecration and sacrifice

architect of light vessels

the girl who chews at obedience
like a leather strap

thermometer
mercury
element
atom

Eve

[2012]

Psalm

O, Father of all these curious feet,
of all the motherless ones—
I am the asking sort of woman.

Make peace with my poor spirit,
and my thoughts, wandering these thirsty mazes
in search of lullabies and forgotten lines.

How I limp along in looking,
reaching out to receive my portion,
only to return the gift in awkward poses.

How I hunger for the shaping sounds
I want to recall from heavenly cradles
and kitchens gone mute.

How I long to dance away from
asthmatic centuries of feminine lostness
in your house of mirrors.

Be merciful to my pure and wounded heart,
to these mournful wondering thoughts.
Take up this veil and let me see

the doors to all these keys.
Sculpt my meek mouth in spirited language,
and, Lord, bid me sing the Mother's song.

[2015]

The Toscano Heresy

What if the Holy Ghost were She?
If She were who remained with me?
She who brooded? She who burned?
She the hearts of fathers turned?
She the Blessing? She the Power?
She the Knower of the hour?

What if that Holy, Heav'nly Three
Is Godly Him and Him and She?

[2012]

Song to be sung in times of famine, fear, and desolation

(Notes on Helaman 11)

O Father, make it rain.
O Mother, make it quick.
Pour out that balm again
And swift unsick what's sick.

O Lord, our hearth and home,
Cry havoc, wrack, and death:
Send saviors to us soon,
Loose our abated breath,

Cut cutting to the quick,
Pour out that Son again.
O Father, heal the sick.
O Mother, make it rain.

[2013]

The River You Always Knew

She comes unbidden tonight,
while fireflies light the garden,
bleeding hearts glow, crickets
sing your unborn child to sleep.
She moves amid trees,
grows roots beneath hearth.
She is wisdom in your dreams.

She summons errant sons,
unbinds her daughters' tongues,
welcomes the prodigal home.
She sets a table for the feast of
His coming; builds fire, burns chaff,
grinds grain to fine flour.

She mends the day—sews dawn to dusk,
midnight to the falling stars.
She is the river you always knew,
the fountain from which you drink;
a whisper at the kitchen sink when,
outside, around the corner,
your child falls and skins his knee.

She is the lullaby you hum, the song
you sing because your mother knew it.
She is your voice bearing witness
on a certain Sabbath and, just now,
as sunlight crests the mountain,
She is your face in the mirror.

[2013]

Heavenly Mother Sings

hymns hidden in the heart
melodies we hum
nursing babies

wind in the garden
music made of grape vines
cherry blossoms

ballad of comfort in sea-swell for
sailors thrown to knees
requiem on mountain top for
climbers grown cold

she pulls our heartstrings
tunes them to hers and to
her son who sings with us
a song of redeeming love.

[2014]

Mother's Milk

I miss Her breast today;
her heart, pulsing
against my cheek.

She unlatched me;
gave me to the care
of my brother,

her firstborn son.
She is weaning me and
I am weeping mother's milk.

[2014]

A Woman Scorned

It's no use
the voices say
you'll never find her—

> while men in suits
> (convinced she is dead)
> consume the child she bore
> in the wilderness.

Listen. You can hear her
coming, humming—
fury is her lullaby.

[2014]

Word of God

Scriptures of The Father are engraved
on mountains, bound in gold,
trumpeted to the masses
from atop granite
battlements.

> The scriptures of The Mother
> are written in a song book
> in heaven, where only
> a listening heart
> will hear.

[2014]

I Thought I Saw Her

What if I need her right now to
help me write these words?
Will she? Has she?
I can't say for sure.

What I can say is this:
when my husband falls asleep
his hand heavy on my belly
his breath slow and deep
I think she speaks to him
in dreams …

because, when I met him
all the doors in my heart
flew open and for a moment
I thought I saw her in his eyes.

[2016]

How Long the Call

Because the chapel I inhabit
invites no female to the rostrum,

because (they say) my voice
was made for lullabies alone,

because this world proclaimed
another sex the Minister-Leader,

God weeps.

She wails on good days,
sends famine on the bad;

She rends the earth with
floods of blood

and water.

Because they do not hear
The Word, my one word (yes)

echoes through wood
and bones: Catacombs

where every woman saint
waits entombed in silence.

[2017]

Mother Work

If you were born
you've done it

(or given
birth or cried)

this work is yours
and always was

alone or in community
because that is where

She comes when
we ask in silence

in prayer in waiting
for Her voice

Her image
in the Son

this work
this Mother Work

will save us as surely
as the cross and

His blood
in the garden.

[2017]

Mother

Heavenly Mother! Your child
Is sacrificed high up on a cross.

Cry a mother's tears for us—
Mothers who cannot save their children.

Cry for every infant grown old enough to die
Alone without his mother's tears for solace.

Cry for those who lived without heart ... cry ...
Since common children live from their mothers' tears,

And tears of common mothers are used up
Long before their children's final need of them.

[2013]

My Father's Sister

Indifferent to deaths they cause,
men occupy the earth like an army—
wanting to belong to the place they stole.
The curious wings of their burdened brows
hover above pews in this tender chapel
where they yearn for the embrace
of our merciful Mother held in heaven.

A white-haired woman prays here,
huddling in an aged heart,
hair sparse like petals of a flower
brought outside the genetic order.
She kneels and folds in a man's
worn trousers and checkered vest—
her dead husband's, I muse—
his belt gripping her strangled waist.

Far away yet vivid in my mind,
my father's sister lays on her deathbed—
she scratches the earth with her beak
like a bird just fallen from its branch,
pointing to the unseen with a coiled finger.

I remember the day her mother was buried.
She long grieved like an orphan:
"How are we to live until we return
to the care of our Mother above?" she asked.
"With each familiar person I lost
the world has increased with the chilled
blank faces carried by strangers
whose eyes slump, narrow and dull
when I pass them by on gray pavements."

[2014–15]

The Scribe

The lone scribe sits
near blue rocks by the ocean,
lilies and snapdragons in hand—
he will bring them for the Heavenly Mother
when he comes home.

How odd this devotion from a creature—
a man bearing flowers who lights a candle—
sparks a flame in place of an idea—
watches it tremble and beckon.

So many come in this silence,
leave in silence, return to their silence.
It is best to bow, to bend, to kneel,
uncomprehending, but grateful still,
delighted with the imprisonment we call Life—
flesh for which we care abundantly.

What do they see of us
from the other side of the veil,
caught as we are in a proper divide,
carried by this earth and the sounds of drums—
primal, unavoidable—that penetrate the womb
beyond the night, beyond enclosures, beyond silence,
past faded flowers of a receding past, and reach us here
in the peace implanted in us like a resurrection?

[2014–15]

the God particle

In the uppermost corner
of the tallest glass window
in the draftiest laboratory
the marble moon hangs,
a little round note in a vast
conservatory of light.

On a spindly metal stool
she perches, hunches over
her notes, strands of brown
gossamer escaping her hasty
bun. A whiff of sulfur seeps
into her nostrils and flees
away on a gust of wind.

"This formula you have drawn—
it is not quite right," she muses. "We created
it in the lab before. It did not form
any useful material. Do you remember?"

Do you remember, echoes across the
room, dashing light years through a
grand canyon of stars.

He pauses, pricked, and continues
his wild scramble across regions of
blackboard.

A trail of chalky equations ripples
beneath his hand. Lines and letters
and integers spark as thought coils
into substance and—almost—motion.

In the beginning, they met in this lab.
He can picture it in every twinkling
corner of his mind. Beakers glinting,
glasses filled with infinite mystery.

And, then, to look on her.

Infinitesimal movement of air.
Infinitesimal breath of knowing.
Infinitesimal beat of heart.
Infinitesimal sweet and start.

What once was not, now is.
What once was void is now light.
What once was calm is raging sea.
What once was satisfaction is insatiety.
What once was inhale is now exhale.
What once was loss is now perfection.

It is creation.

I am trying to describe a thing without
form or weight. Delicious and holy,
a substance that will fill all space.

She feels his thoughts. She holds him in her
mind and heart, even when she is with him,
and feels she knows something of his way,
although at times it is beyond her grasp.

She simply feels the power, the sumptuous
greening in her heart when she looks on him,
robed in light, walking amid his many creations.

I have seen him answer the question that
chased him for centuries: When will the
universe be organized? When will we uncover
the pattern infallible with which to charm
chaos?

They are ἄτομος. They are one.

[2013]

Mothers in Heaven

> *I always write as if to my mother.*
> —Ted Kooser

What shall I say to my mother today?
How is heaven after sixty-four years?
You'd be ninety-three on earth,
crinkled, complaining about your back,
forgetting where you put your teeth.

But I see your golden hair
in a perfect 1940's bob,
you, pink as your chenille robe,
seated on a chrome kitchen chair.

Curious, what a four-year-old absorbs,
what soaks into the soul like permanent dye:
      your hugs in the night
      when the Terribles came to visit,
      or hand in hand
      skips around the block
      singing Skip to my Lou,
      giggles
      when an old lady parted her curtains.

With your absence, another curtain parted
in my motherless hours. I sensed
the nearness of the Mother we once knew,
the Heavenly One who sent us off to earth
much as we send our little ones off to class,
with tears, prayers and hands held to the last.

How is school in heaven, Mom?
One day we'll share a desk,
learn the mother's art
from the One who knows it best.

[2014]

I think the sky may be a woman— See how
she spoons into cumulus— How she vessels
the death-rush of Eurus like uterus vessels
flesh, fleshes soul, flushes placenta crimson
and supple as solitude— How she slips into
azure, ritual, heraldry ancient as Eden's backdrop,
heaven breaking at her breast, shearing
her vestments sheer as cirrostratus at dusk—

Let her vespers hushed as flesh-hum in desire's
half-light lure you through her veil into holiest flesh—
Cleanse your soul in her laver brimful with desire—
Trace her constellations devout as the subtle vault
of her skin, devout as the pull and release of her name
slipping again and again from his tongue—

(After Brian Kershisnik)

[2014]

Goddess Sonnets

(After J. Kirk Richards)

i.
Goddess looking up, sowing mercy
in the shadow she broadcasts like seed,
left hand sifting the infinite satchel she wears
at her hip, fingers praying each grain
as she yields them to soil. On the valley's
blank page, they punctuate
the language of wind, shape its words
into clauses the trees can understand.

As she sows, first light parts the mist, whispers
her name. Right hand to cheek, she translates
the matins' caress into the psaltery
of her skin. Her body sings azure the tone
of a mourning dove's elegy across the cosmos
she upholds with her dreams.

[2015]

ii. Goddess dreaming of her temple in the woods,

dreaming haze-draped aspen, an earthen laver,
light settling like the sweetness and ardor of oil,
verdure spreading like worship, incense
embroidering updrafts like epiphany;

savoring the mourning doves' devotion,
the sparrows' allelu, the bluebirds' psalm
and selah, quail chanting their anxious reveille,
grouse thrumming to the hum of her ecstasy;

eavesdropping on the grove's droning lull,
sidling up to its mystery, undressing its shadows
like flames stripping cosmos to praise on the Makers'
earthen shrine, whispering her name into flesh
as it rises to greet wind, saying, "Here: take
this body, my beloved, my longing, my tongue—"

[2014]

iii. Goddess in repose

                       : at rest, perhaps
late the seventh day, body settling
into the sigh she released the moment
the universe slipped from her womb,
sidled up to the Infinite, began suckling
from its teat—
                       : mid-vision, perhaps,
as the universe sighs, whispers its fortune
into the worlds she inhabits like skin—

                       : mid-garden, mid-
bliss, trees blushing in Eden's rapture
as she arches into sky to shade
Eden's exiles on their lone walk through
wilderness, as she whispers them
dream-ward, whispers them beyond—

[2015]

iv. Goddess choosing her fruit

It's in the way she caresses each rind as she
wanders the market, pausing to read the secrets
raised like braille from cantaloupe, to tell
the vined heirlooms, to interpret the quince;
in the way she carries her basket, brim with
grapes, maybe olives, the handle looped
around her arm, hanging loose from her elbow,
the cradle held snug by her earthward palm;
in the way she's shifted her weight to one leg,
hips anticipating a turn toward the women
tending pomegranates near the entrance,
their voices beatifying the breeze, unfolding
a cosmos-deep incantation as they palm
each globe into the urgency of dawn—

[2017]

v.

Goddess stirring something up, folding light
into cosmos the way her mother showed her
an aeon ago   *cradle the bowl between torso*
and forearm   the bowl's weight in one palm,
divining rod clasped in the other, fold the mix
to a loose whorl   closing her eyes, she steps
toward the memory, pauses, cocks her head
to listen to the crack of life shifting the mixture

her first time with the recipe, the crack shook
the bowl from her grasp   *steady against*
the shift   bowl to belly, lean into your mixing
and eavesdrop on the batter as it swells to
emergence   feel it clench just before release
let it sputter   let it pulse   let it   breathe

[2017]

Phoning Home

I called to talk with Mom
but Dad was on the other end
and would speak for her.

>   (The Germans have a word for it:
>   *Fürsprecher*)

But really,

I'd rather speak right to her, not through you, I joked
—not wanting to be ugly or difficult or to snub him—
so he put us on speaker phone.

Her voice was a formless whimper.

"Can she speak any louder? Or maybe if you
put the phone to her ear—"
"Here!" wanting to be helpful he
stretched the receiver her direction

>   (The Norwegians have a word for it:
>   *Ordfører*)

Relaying all my every word (and hers) in his
amplified
supermarket
public announcement system
echo.

But actually,

I don't want a mole carrying my word (or hers)—

> (The French have a word for it:
> *Porte parole*)

No intermediary, please, if I could
just speak
if she could
just speak
if she would just be the one on the other end when I call
to talk with Mom.

[2014]

Of Thy Womb

My Catholic husband prays
the Hail Mary over the body
of our baby, who has arrived at home—
without warning and far too early.

So early that Sam says
he looks like a boxer,
his tiny fists up to his face,
his eyes like black beads.

I ache for my own Hail Mary—
some mothering, mourning prayer.
I'm emptying, Godless, thinking
of Her as we drive to the hospital,

of Mother in Heaven, wondering whether
half-organized souls ever dissipated,
split from her without warning,
left her in grief.

While I wait to be hollowed I use Father
as a messenger to reach Her, if I may.
But perhaps it's no use.

She's not at my bedside, shimmering
in empathetic sorrow when I wake. She's not
there at the edges of me, or at the emptied center.
But maybe She's in the voice of the nurse who mothers
me back to consciousness and helps me sip water.
Perhaps She's in the water, in the stack of white pillows,
in the heated blankets tucked around me.

And perhaps She's in Sam's hand
as he passes it over my forehead,
gently as a prayer.

[2014]

O

This my only prayer to you: a mouth wide open.
Hunger and thirst are my loud song, my silence.
In woe and joy, I call to you, in sow and sorrow.
O let me grow. O let me reach your fruited bough.
No word is full until you teach me how to speak.
O let me kneel at your powerful knee. O let me feel
Your strong, sweet-smelling fingers cup my face.
O that you would hold my chin up and teach me
Your language. I would memorize your teeth and tongue,
Your stretching, pursing mouth, the way
Your throat moves. O you who no one names.
December Woman. Tenth Month Lady. Deep Mother.
The Earth is yours and every growing thing says your name.

[2014]

My Mother Is . . .

My mother is the ocean—
The color of an eye, edged in foamy lace.
She is an equal partner to heaven—
As she negotiates rainfall with the sky.

My mother is the earth—
Covered in a quilt of terrain and water.
She creates our daily bread—
As she nurtures seeds in her moist, dark flesh.

My mother is the moon—
A pale faced beauty, cold and hard.
She lifts up blood and water—
As she curves her shape into sacred patterns.

My mother is the shadow—
Subtle like shading, yet equal to light.
She gives us our vision—
As she mixes colors with depth.

My mother is me—
Our essence flows from the same source.
We connect to oneness—
As we weave tapestries of truth.

[2014]

To Her

I sometimes attempt escape,
These days, in the rasp
Of autumn winds unraveling in my head
Like old, neglected violins;
In my grief, I can travel between worlds.
As with rain cupped in the dying hands
Of leaves, the sunset alchemically coalesces into rose-gold
Champagne in the pools of my eyes
Like stories told in stained glass
Of fallen angels longing
In darkness for everlasting light—that which
Simultaneously torments and exalts.
Beyond some abstract ideal, or some outrageously-proportioned
Fertility symbol, you are as tangible as I
Passing with me beneath the boughs of trees,
Your breath, the susurrations of the leaves
As something inside you speaks to something within me
In a language that exfoliates, from Winter, perennial Spring.
Your unrecognized presence recalls light that flickers
In darkness while the darkness does not comprehend it,
And yet, in the liminal space between night and
Daybreak the long grass clings to your thighs as
You dance, blanketing the ground beneath your feet
With its glistening hair while the dew that
Collects on its strands hardens
Into stars that confess that you go on and on,
Enthroned amid a sea of fire and glass.

[2014]

Yin

White Father administers,
we go to Him in our time of need.
We attempt gratitude
so He will act in our favor.

Black Mother is hidden,
we forget Her every time.
We attempt nothing
because we do not care to know.

Yin and yang
but the moon is not passive,
following and guiding simultaneously.
Every line affects the next.

The other half of God can be found
and She will act of Her own accord,
for God is a bystander
until called upon.

[2014]

Veil

It is difficult to see through
    the boiling water. The slats in the wood spoon
wave and disappear as I scoop the ladle
    under the macaroni sticking to its siblings
and the pot that holds my focus.

    Some mothers would warn to mind the fire,
some to use the fan above the stove,
    but Mother does not use her voice. I hear her
from the pantry or behind me by the island,
    all her happiness moving my direction
the way sound moves through water—
    I need only be its destination.

Before the need to move away from home,
    before my words and fingers pushed her back,
before the idea of an independent self
    settled on my psyche, I was known.
This woman has seen behind me, seen me
    grow into my body, felt my hunger, quenched my flame.
The house has changed. Not all the doors are open
    yet. Feeling my way forward I find traces of her
essence when I press against the walls.

[2014]

Rejoinder

If Eve is any indication
one need not go far
in speculation to assume
the woman holding God's hand
has seen it all before
her long ago. She is past
and future, She relegates
the here and now to He
who lives in the moment
who fills with breath
who rides the lightning
until the all familiar fingers
rest on His to say it is
enough and guide them quiet
into the coming day.
She is how He sees
it is good. She is opposition
in its purest sense: a way
to be what is not and what is,
a way to note each sparrow's fall
and know its name as well.
As each body settles into earth
She calls what rises home.

[2014]

Misting Eden

From the other side of the room,
stars flash into being like sparks from a wheel
and are placed (artistically as well as functionally)
close enough to see each other, but just.
Not the workshop you expected to see,
the woman's studio strikes you as small.
Enclosed she would say. There are color wheels
in the corner, fragments of a new flower's throat
she hasn't gotten around to. Tables and tables
of handwritten math stacked below the window,
and through the glass, her masterpiece, the moon.
If you shut the door, something dangles in a frame:
the first raindrop ever made (she invented water,
insisted on misting Eden herself). Walking backward
through what you would call a mess, she doesn't
stumble once, keeping her eye on the charcoal sketch
of a long-necked bird you'd never recognize.
Talk to me, baby—a whisper at best. At a stretch,
one wing falters and she, knowingly, laughs.

[2015]

Heavenly Mother Eats Carbs

There is nothing lovely left in the body
I have been taught to despise:
measured and found wanting,
tight in my clothes, heavy
with the weight of years and children,
too tethered to the earth.

In the seconds before I turn away
I glimpse Her in my widened hips,
my deflated breasts,
the silver purple lines that map my abdomen:
a sense of power etched across my veins.

But when I turn back,
it's only me
who sees the reflection
who steps off the scale.

[2014]

It's Possible I'm Projecting

I picture Her
a Heavenly Hausfrau:
bare celestial feet,
breasts heavy above an eternally rotund belly.

She's stirring a pot of lentil soup
with a spirit child on each hip
while twelve trillion toddlers crowd Her knees
insisting they won't try it.

Caught between sharp elbows,
She shakes Her sheets early
and showers with an audience.
Her sky is streaks of spilled white milk,
dirty diapers, piles and piles of unmatched socks.
Her Holy hands work while all those children
track mud across Her vast, perpetual carpet.

In a productive rage,
She scrubs and wonders
When was the last time she sat down to a hot meal?
Why does everyone keep rubbing their snotty noses
on Her skirt, Her sleeves, Her skin?

She can't even hide Her Glory in Kolob's bathroom
long enough to eat a beatific cookie in peace
without little fingers searching underneath the door
as shrill voices whimper "choc-lat?"

Please let that just be me.
I'd rather think She's serene, azure.
Twice a day She cleans her paintbrush,
and every night She fills the sky with stars:
lights to calm us.

[2014]

To Stay Forgotten

Mists and Darkness
through the veil:
How many hands have been denied me?
Mothers tessellating unto Him:
a million million to populate the ends
of His creation.

She is egg and yolk and shell:
a perennial blossom, expanding,
the circle of Her broken,
regained and broken again.

She is Herself, one of many.
Atop a pedestal, protected,
unknown, unblessed, uncursed.

[2014]

The Seven Songs of Creation

One.

While He slept, Mother whispered songs and sounds into his ear, all night long, and so it was that the whale opened its mouth undersea and sang and whistled and trilled, its body like a giant cello humming through the ocean, Mother's hand drawing a bowstring across its ribs. And Father said, this is good.

Two.

During the night, She rubbed her legs and feet against His for hours, and elephant erupted in foghorn screams and the females sang a song so low it could not be heard, an infrasound moving through the leg bones of amorous males, the pads of their feet; the males moved towards the booming for love and longevity, some of them standing tip-toed to hear her miles away. And Father said, this is good.

Three.

Mother's voice rose high into the firmament the third night as she pitched her soprano song against the clouds, the moon's bright back, stars. The sounds bounced back and forth through the sky, like bird notes. Before sunrise, bats opened their mouths and echoed each other in the high pitchings of love, a sound so spiked Father had trouble hearing. He said, this is good. I think.

Four.

As they slept, She was exhausted, her breath rising and falling in harmony with His, their night sounds philharmonic, joining and climbing in something like ecstasy. That day God made mosquitoes, male and female, and blessed them, and She taught them to whine, the males high pitched and frenetic, the females at ease, waiting, patient, their wing-beats adjusting in harmony, Father shooing them away with the wind of his hand, thinking perhaps, this wasn't so good.

Five.

She rested her head and hand on His chest and felt the commotion of his heart, His work almost finished, animals running away from His outstretched hand pounding the ground with their hard feet, the grouse thumping the air with its love song, giraffes running miles against the earth's trails without rest, ant feet, horse hooves, antelope, all of them running against the earth into their kingdoms. The next day He created woodpeckers without song, thick-beaked, strong necked, thick skulled; and Mother gave them rhythm and blues, hollow notes, love of the drill and the knock of wood. And God said, yes, this will be okay.

Six.

During the night as she sang to Father, Her arm fell asleep under her head, the numbness calling to Her through the night, fingers rising and falling, thumb outstretched, her blood slowing to a soft warble through her veins. In the morning God created manakins, their red hoods the color of blood, wings of strange feathers and solid bones, scrapers and combs, nervous twitchings and vibrations. She blew into their mouths string notes, rattling their wings faster than sound, tingling, twitching. They raise their wings like small flags and call out, "I'm here. I'm here." And Father said, of course, this is as it should be. But He was tired and wanted rest.

Seven.

During the night, Mother dreamed of Adam and Eve. The serpent in Eden. Eve's apple. The animals fanning out towards desert, forests, mountains, valleys; she saw them opening their mouths, their voices rising from colored throats, some playing their bodies like instruments, notes rising from the oceans and streams. Today when Her man said, this is finished and it's good, she felt defeated, numb, hoarse from giving voice to all creatures, all of them. During the day she lay down and slept, and dreamed, and watched ants and bugs crawl off and fish swim away in their muted bodies.

[2014]

When God Created the Swan

All morning the jeweled birds:
hummings, orioles, buntings
like colored glass, small, cute,
manageable. Mid-morning:
coffee-break coming, boredom,
all turned shades of black,
crow-dull, raven, grackle,
beaks yellow-hued, starling,
or shades of gray and gray-brown
gulls, scaups, and laziness,
quail, cormorants, a multitude
of hawks, ducks, stare of owls,
curlews, lapwings, martins, ptarmigans.
Bigger, faster, bodies filling, wings
grossed out for carriage, angle, speed,
soaring, vultures and condors,
lowland turkeys, big birds
with heads like open sores,
old tennis shoes, slabs of pecked meat,
and potoos—flying mouths and eyes—
more fur than feather, the melancholy
wail of the male.

At noon He walks slump-shouldered
from the shop in a burned-out drabness
like gray, to the house, to the kitchen,
to Mother, making soup, her grace,
the long line of her neck, every movement
like birdsong, the fierce whiteness
of her skin, her eyes lazuli blue, crystal.
He naps and dreams of wings, tip feathers
curling in flight, clouds of bats, grist of bees,
flamingoes, herons, pheasants. And
then, something curved, willowy,
the line of his wife's neck falling
to her shoulder, her waist, roundness,
fullness, feathers lighter than water,
unhurried, a floating shiver of white,
voice like an oboe, and, ah the face,
His wife looking towards him over her shoulder.

[2014]

The Woman Whose Husband Finds Heart-Shaped Stones

They pulse and throb and wait for him,
in the dirt, in piles, in streams, on hillsides,
and once one waited
its whole rock-heart-life for him
on a fence post
near Cody, Wyoming,
who knows, maybe hundreds of years.

She held one up
at the podium where she spoke
to make sure we understood
and even from the thirteenth pew
I could see it.
I could feel it beating in her hand.
I could hear him calling her name
as the door closed behind him
at 11:00 pm, the heart in his hand,
and she knew it was coming with him
through the door.

And I believed. I wanted to rise
and walk forward, wanted to stand at the podium
and bear witness of the heart-shaped-rock,
to say from where I sat I could feel it
beating in her hand. But when I looked
down the rows, pew after pew,
people had their heads down,
some texted or held their iPods,
a few of the older ones slept.

Days now, and regret. Nothing from the pulpit
had turned my own heart like this:
The ten commandments, Joshua and Jericho,
staffs parting water, Mother and Father
creating the world, animals, birdsong,
the Book of Eli. Nothing.

And slowly something hard and cold
takes shape in my chest, and it will get, I know,
so heavy, that one day soon
it will drop its way through my bowels,
and when they come to drag me away,
it will lie in the dirt waiting.

[2014]

Eloher

You caterpillar across the page
of our thoughts. Flight is imminent.
Wings are more than metaphor.
If Father is sun, and Son is moon,

You are salt on a black tablecloth.
You season everything, hurtle millions
of light years to be near
us. You are spores, snowflakes, particles

of yellow pollen. You are aspen saplings,
diamonds forged in darkness, grains of sand
under oyster tongues. You're neutrons,
You're seafoam, You're motes of dust

spinning in a shaft of afternoon light.
We're mammal, still look for you against our cheek.
We're marsupial, barely weaned from the pouch.
We're reptile, straining against the skin of our eggs

to reveal Your face.

[2014]

Harvest Dance

From cloud cloth she cuts a fabric fine and tinseled,
edges soaked in wine and white middled. Needled
pine she pins to pattern, runs through with silver river
threaded line. When done, a full skirt she sets on
mountain mannequin till Michaelmas and the harvest
dance. Then watch her spin and spin across the sky.
Rivers flash like lightning. Her bare feet smashing
as she heel-toe-heel-toes it across a field of rye.
Father's there stomp-clapping, keeping time.
They hook elbows, dancing "Drops of Brandy," book it
right over the county line, His & Hers, yours & mine.

[2014]

DAYNA PATTERSON

Mother Has a Degree in Exterior Design

See how she offsets the Prussian blue of the bay
by its opposite on the color wheel,
the splendid burnt orange of a just-so sunset

And see how that lemon wedge of sun
draws the eye,
makes the colors pop

And over here—see how she's hung drops of dew
like a little string of holiday lights
on a spider's web

And see how the spider's pendulous body
droops like a gold earring
on the web's lobe

She's not afraid to use
every shade of green:
forest, shamrock, olive, jungle

She adores red:
hoodoos she hordes like knick knacks
in the cupboard of a Utah desert

Look up—see how she mixes and matches
edgy patterns of birds that verge on chaotic
with classic clouds and bolts of blue

And look how she arranges
all those migrants into Sanskrit
to make a prayer wheel of the sky

[2014]

Whale Watching

The morning's fog is thick as frosted glass.
Every wave's shadow and sea-drifting log
breathes innuendo. Strain eyes to their limits, ears
perched alert for the spurt of water to signal

their surfacing. A pod of females follow her
through the Salish Sea, hunting for seals and salmon.
Walk the half-mile trail south to north, north
to south, south to north. Commandeer a picnic bench

and wait, unpack sandwiches, stare at water,
and don't dare let your eyes wander.
Hike up to the lighthouse and wait.
Hike down to the old kiln and wait.

Seals. Moss. Purple starfish big as backpacks.
Pull out binoculars. Cameras. And wait.
Watch for her girl's club, imagine her sleek
dorsal fin higher than our heads, her black back

like a moving hill, weaving in and out of water,
sewing big stitches in the dark blue bay.
She's circling round these islands
where we live our little lives.

Her massive grace. Her godsome body.

[2014]

New Moon

Mother, you are new moon

Reveal your glorious face

Give us Mother-knowledge soon

A sliver here and there

That we may bear

The waxing of your light

Till we attain a fullness of your grace

To guide us through mortality's night

[2014]

Creation Story

Mother & Father said let there be light
and there was light
      comet light porch light torch light
      lamp light campfire light pyre light
           light of marine phosphorescence
           light of the moon in a crescent
           light of a firefly cloud

Father & Mother said let there be dark
and there was dark
      negro dark tornado dark cave dark
      mind dark blind dark grave dark
           dark of the sickroom
           dark of the red velvet womb
           dark of the Mariana Trench

Mother & Father said let there be music
and there was music
      frog music bog music thunder music
      cricket music moon music loon music
           music of roof rain
           music of fire logs crackling
           music of humpback whales

Father & Mother said let there be dance
and there was dance
          flamingo dance flamenco dance rain dance
          red crane dance wind dance grain dance
                    dance of courtship
                    dance of worship
                    dance of cell mitosis

Mother & Father said let there be color
and there was color
          dolphin blue crab red starfish purple
          orange orange yolk yellow petal pink
                    color of sun-bleached bones
                    color of sixteen stones
                    color of Noah's hope

Father & Mother said let there be love
and there was love
          puppy love frozen love Higgs boson love
          cousin love mosquito love burrito love
                    love of a thousand words
                    love of eggless birds
                    love of bleeding hearts blooming

[2014]

DAYNA PATTERSON

If Mother Braids a Waterfall

in a country where no one speaks
her language   if She's a queen
few bow to, few supplicate   if She's a book

no one reads, verses
rich as incantation   if Mother weaves a forest
floor from tree roots in a swath of clear

cut   if She untangles rivers into tributary
threads, the beds long since dry
if She's a gold rush with no prospectors   if

She's a queen bee with no drones, honeycomb
without attendants   if in the morning, Mother conducts
a chorus of larks   if at night, a throng of nightingales

if Her children sleep through the song   if She holds a rope
through an oubliette's trapdoor, calls
down to us, but we focus on the guard

who pushes grub through the bean slot
once a day, his thrilling fingertips, his footstep echoing
as he walks away   if we look up at last   if we relearn Mother

Tongue through hard listening   if She's an awaiting
-rain arroyo, a golden seam for our broken
pottery, a worship-worthy starscape

[2017]

ELISA EASTWOOD PULIDO

Sightings:
The Heavenly Mother in North Central Texas

1.

I saw Her twenty years ago at the Grand Opening
of a Tom Thumb Page in Carrolton. She
was in the frozen food section, performing
Brahms on a cold white grand, surrounded
by frozen broccoli and turkey burgers.
Blonde hair piled high, arms like cannons, She wore
a red formal, red lips, a double strand of pearls.

Oh Goddess of the flash freeze, and the quickie meal!
If I had cried out to You right there in aisle number 8,
Would You have taken me to your ample bosom? Would You
have told me truly that Life is both high culture and TV dinners?

2.

Two years ago, She was in the children's chapel
of the Plano 9th Ward. Aged four, She delivered
a wee sermon on Christ's love for his creatures.
She hadn't a clue—soteriology, eschatology, missiology,
demonology, angelology, the history of the Church,
the tenets of the faith—passed Her completely by.
No matter. Her Mother whispered prompts; She echoed them.

Oh Heavenly Mother! If I had implored You right there
at the children's pulpit to remove my doubt, would You have said,
"Patience! All will be revealed," or, would You have repeated
     words
whispered by yet another Mother, and would it have mattered?

          3.
Last year, I saw her wiping tables
at a bakery on Preston Road, Her hands
hastily gathered dirty plates and soiled napkins.
The salvific miracle of Her gray rag and spray bottle
filled with lemon-scented disinfectant, rescued
customers from the plague, this year's flu,
hoof and mouth—whatever else might ail us.

Oh Queen of the menial wage! I am surrounded by all that is
     unclean.
If I had dropped to my knees right next to Your janitorial caddy,
Would You have swept Texas free of the unworthy image,
Would you have wiped bigotry and greed off the counter?

          4.
I was with her at the Collin County Courthouse,
yesterday. Attorneys deliberated Her financial fate.
She'd been cast off like a squeezed lemon.
Wearing a tweed suit, a thin gold chain,
She meditated on divorce. Hands folded, eyes closed,
imperturbable as the Buddha, She accepted
that the life She had known was over. Selah.

Oh Heavenly Consort! If I am ever abandoned and pleading
my case in the Collin County or some other courthouse,
rouse Yourself, slam Your fists on some table, any table,
and swear to me that all will be well, and all will be well.

[2014]

The Heavenly Mother Takes a Break

Sometimes it is all too much,
and even a mother of gods
may grieve under pressure.

This is when the Heavenly Mother
makes an appearance in her pumpkin-colored coach.
At the drive-through window of a fast-food joint
at the edge of the galaxy, she orders a diet Coke.

This grieving is only because
Mothers want so much.

And, no matter how bountiful the worlds,
Her children tend to live out their days in squalor:

In a neighboring yard,
a tomato vine has escaped its cage;
its fruit rots on the ground.

Fog from a nearby beach has begun
to peel paint from the sills
of community windows.

Overhead, a constellation of gulls falls
from the sky and settles in soiled napkins,
cast-off fries, and burger buns discarded
on the black top. A one-legged gull
hops through the detritus.

There is an excess in maternal hope
that borders on folly.

Let this folly
be our teacher.

Inside the restaurant mothers and children
in party hats eat ice cream and cake.

They are mustard weeds sprouting
through cracks in the universe
where they sing and make wishes
before blowing out the lights.

[2015]

Windows

I used to go out for a walk,
and speak to the night's cyclopean eye and its freckled face.
I thought I might woo God, the Woman in the Moon,
out of Her hiding place where She spies
on mortals with an enormous telescope.

I kept thinking if I buzzed long enough
like cicadas on my trees in muggy evenings
She, like Christ's unjust judge,
might grow weary and give me a wink or a blush,
or even a rude gesture to let me know of Her affections.

But sign-seeking grew boring—
I tired of dolling up Her silence as an answer,
or seeing symbols of Her stitched in nature's quilt,
in patches of trees, eggs, or bees,
so I buttoned up the soul I'd laid bare and sauntered off.

Imagine my surprise when I arrived
home with a parcel man at the door,
who had me sign for a package containing a trilby hat,
a pile of rocks, and a note telling me I'd know what to do.

God may have a knack for enlivening,
lighting, and enlarging stones,
but I still felt foolish as I dropped them
in the hat's crown on the off chance
of a heavenly peep, Siddharthan enlightenment, or practical joke.

No beloved apostle's apocalypse.
No picturesque panorama as presented to Nephi.
I had every right to be disappointed,
when I noticed looking on a stone in the hat
spun my mind's wheel and had its needle fall on a memory:

The leopard's heavy paw that woke me
from addiction's stupor on a Namibian night,
The voice by which I sang the gospel's
joyous blues to Cajuns and crawfish,
The course I'd sailed through reason's meandering maths.

As I dwelt on words with which
I blessed my twiceborn son,
Eliza's secret something, the christened muse,
wrapped me in its radiant wreath and whispered,
These are windows through which shines Her grace.

[2014]

A Visit Like Any Other

At the rustic fence She stood, dressed with years,
Bent and twisted like an Australian snow gum,
Life's white wine blossoming on Her cheeks,
And wisdom scribbled in Her every wrinkle.
Her hand rested on rickety gate
As She herded in her wild brood,
Which hooted along a mulch footpath,
Surged up the stairs of a Farmhouse porch,
And so lustily hounded after
The cinnamon scent of Father's bread
That they nearly forgot to shed their sandals.

It was a visit like any other:
Time filled with the sacraments of
Loud laughter, besting kids at cards and dice,
Building model aircraft, and painting *alla prima*.
On Mitchell's request, She read a Classic:
Gaulpieri's tale of a cursed thief
Whose stolen items lost all value.
Fineries would not sell, food ceased
To nourish or taste, art did not please.
The moral of the story (if there was one)
Lost on the infant minds.
All this followed by the inevitable nap on the floor
Next to contented fat Labradors,
Puddling on one another like a pod of walruses.

And when the Sun, blushing with exertion,
Could no longer hold himself up,
She gathered the family outside
Round a creamy lemon picnic bench by
Potted plants posing on window sills.
She unearthed a hefty tome of lives,
Each yellow, crinkled leaf holding
Faded pictures of relatives long since departed.
The children, looming anxiously over,
Pointed at family and jabbered:
"Tell the story of when Anchu rode a bunjuback!
Did Wilhemina ever learn to sing?
I wanna hear Zuly's jokes again."

She smiled and glanced eastward, Her mind
Vaulting over the frozen music of mountains,
Over the veiled horizon, and the snow of space,
To find Her other sheep bleating, grazing at food trucks,
Head butting, hoof stomping in offices,
And engaging in all number of ovine behaviors.
Then obliging the inquests of this young flock,
She wondered what tales
They might add to the chronicle
Before they went the way to the earth.

[2015]

Prayers of Gods

I.

Sometimes I wonder if Gods pray, and not from former habit.
I cannot see how eternity's swell stills the hunger for reverence.

Do Mother and Father bend the knee on amber cobblestones,
vacate footwear, and press fluorescent faces to frozen seas of glass?
Perhaps They wrap speech in awkward formality,
light candle wicks, dance, or stretch hands above Their heads?

I wonder to whom our Parents sigh for peace.
Would They howl to the never full moon glory of ever-higher powers,
or hike to the summit of Gods and lay Their plight at Grandparents'
    feet?

But then I ask what might the throne bearers do?
Nod to conjoined twins Matter-Mind,
or turn inward and bury Themselves in mantras?
Might Each reside in the sanctuary of the Other?

Or when Gods cannot look up or across,
do They peer down the well of being,
throw in Their buckets,
and plead with all below to fill them?

As when Adam was blest by his sons,
might Mother and Father be blest by children?

II.

If a coroner took a shiv to Mother's prayer, what might he find inside?
Would he unearth praises to the richness of being?
Or might he discover terrified pleas for advice,

that She had kneaded and rolled out the amorphous jelly of Her will,
not knowing what Her will was, or whether it should be done?
(Sandy might deserve a bike, but should Harold leave his unfaithful
    wife?)

Would the autopsy reveal Father prays for resolve to not throw off
    His mantle
and beam through space like angels in conduits of light?
Or that He debates the propriety of taking a furlough to recreational
    nebulae,
allowing deists and epicurists to be right about the apathy of Gods
    for a season?

[2017]

Gardens of Stories

What do we really know about
our heavenly mother?
Nothing except what reason claims.
A vast blanket of sacred silence
rests over her like a veil
until some future day we meet.
But when nothing is known
the human mind scatters seeds
of speculation and gardens of stories
crop up to fill our emptiness
and heal our loneliness.

Here is a story I will tell for myself:
She will slip down here
some evening on a whim,
not as goddess, but as mother
who remembers me from when
I pushed against the cup of her
glorified bone--even before
I took my first cold breaths
of celestial air, and she will
come in the form of a moon,
and spread her light over me.

She will climb through my bedroom
window and hop into my bed
and wake me. Hold me in her arms,
tell me all she hopes for me.
Hum that song she might have hummed
before I was formed in the belly.
She will kiss me on what's left
of my hair and promise
that before too long
I will get to come home to her
when all of this is finished.

[2014]

A Mother's Comfort

A dear friend writes to me of the pain of a child gone too soon—
Not even arrived enough to be gone—
Of the feeling of something slipping through your fingers
No matter how hard you grasp it,
Of joy turned to sorrow turned to hope turned to ash,
And it flees on the wind at will with the wisdom you thought you had.
A mother's pain
Needs a Mother's comfort.

A sister cries over the phone about the disparity
Between the life she imagined and the one in front of her.
"I never knew it would be this hard," she says.
Three small mouths, making heard small voices that
Need need need.
Be careful what you wish for, be grateful for what you have—no,
A mother's pain
Needs a Mother's comfort.

A desperate friend searches the wide world
For something she was promised if only she would obey,
And obey she has, and yet
That promise sits unfulfilled in some other girl,
Some other bed, some other life,
And she's left to hope that somewhere some girl
Will slip up,
Forget to obey,

And want to make it right.
A mother's pain
Needs a Mother's comfort.

A grandmother looks at her children grown
And feels she's failed them—
Look how hard their lives are!
How much pain could I have prevented?
How much did I cause?
How sad not to have your regrets at the beginning
When you still have the chance to change.
A mother's pain
Needs a Mother's comfort.

In a dimly lit room in the dead of night
Where I rock and I rock and I rock,
I see his sweet face and feel his sweet tongue—
And I'm stopped by a love so deep and a pain so sharp
To know that these nights will pass
And, for us, there will be no more sweet faces.

I cry out without sound to Him I've been told is there,
But my soul yearns for something more.
He knows my pain, yes,
But so does She. And
A mother's pain
Needs a Mother's comfort.

[2014]

Flesh and Bones

The mythos of my childhood is filled with flesh and bones.

My newly formed conscience
rocked in the cradle of a Judeo-Christian world
made from Earth.
Formed from the clay, Adam would return,
ashes to ashes and dust to dust,
only bones remaining.
All who enter this world,
only bones remaining.

Yet, from Adam's bones came Eve: the Rib.
An arc of bone protecting the heart,
the heart that beats time with
a world made of earth:
the tides, the seasons, the flesh which returns and the
bones which remain.
The rib, an arc of bone protecting the lungs,
the lungs that inspire the breath of life: Spirit.

Eve, from bone made flesh,
The Mother of All Living.
Eve, beloved archetype,
a tangible version of Mother in Heaven
envisioned by the prophetess Eliza,
misappropriated as a beguiled sinner

whose melancholic whistle sounds through
the dry bones of patriarchy.

I know better, cradled as I was in the myth
of a world made of Earth.

I am of the land, like Adam, like Eve.
I am of the land that nourished and sustained
a ragtag band of Saints who envisioned
a Mother God to rival that of a Father,
who settled on Ute soil already deemed sacred:
Mother Earth.

This is the Mother I understand,
the Mother whose presence inhabits
forest cathedrals,
her song from clear running brooks.
Her call to worship: the sun and the moon,
the cycle of birth and death,
ashes to ashes and dust to dust,
only bones remaining.

Yet nothing to fear, She whispers,
this earth made flesh and flesh made earth,
this yielding of elements
merely a requisite for renewal and rebirth.

Mine is the mythos of Mother, in all her iterations.

[2014]

I Dreamed I Wrote Five Poems

I.

I searched for my Mother, the way a baby roots
for her mother's breast, head nuzzling from side to side,
mouth open, ready to suckle. But I was still thirsty.
Then my belly grew, and my breasts grew, and
a ravenous little thing came out. I offer her my milk
without money and without price. My husband
offered it to her once, while I sat beside them on a train.
She pursed her lips against the false nipple,
and stared at me with sad eyes. I wondered then,
if Heavenly Mother walked into another room
so we would take the bottle. I wondered then,
if we are weaned.

II.

The Father could not hear
His daughter's whimpering,
though He slept beside her
in the same room.
He could not hear her crying,
nor her screaming.
The Mother woke at every sound.

III.

Conch shells.
They are not the ocean;
they are memories of the ocean.
Birds. Trees. Olive oil. Bread. Moons.
They are not the Mother;
they are memories of the Mother.
I hear Her everywhere.

IV.

God's Spirit, God's Breath,
the one He could not live without,
gave me breath when I
gave my daughter life.
She sat beside me on the precipice,
so I would not be alone. We exhaled
and inhaled in unison. She whispered,
calling me by name.

V.

I asked my daughter two questions
the day that she was born.
    1)   Did she remember me—
           my voice, my smell,
           my beating heart?
    2)   Did she remember
           the one we both call Mother—
           Her voice, Her smell, Her heart?
I can't remember anything.

[2014]

Breathe

I tiptoe quietly into my daughter's room,
to see if she's still breathing.
Her chest rises and falls, a hand moves. She sighs.

I tiptoe quietly into my Mother's heaven,
to see if she's still breathing.
Her chest rises and falls, a hand moves. I sigh,
relieved to know God isn't dead.

God tiptoes quietly into my room,
to see if I'm still breathing.
My chest rises and falls, a hand moves. She smiles,
relieved to know I'm sleeping.

[2014]

Postpartum

After creation,
the Mother knew
sorrow—the emptiness
that comes after fullness,
the softness that remains
for a long time.

[2016]

Tree Rings

If we cut Her open,
we could count Her rings
and know Her age,
but we'd also learn Her hunger—
the years She put Her roots down deep
and threw Her arms to the sky,
and how She carried them
with grace.

[2016]

What Rosemary Taught Me

It counts how we
God-talk.
He, Him, His.
She, Her, Hers.
They, Them, Theirs.

It counts how we
God-image.
Almighty father.
Nursing mother.
Partnered parents.

[2017]

First Vision

I walked into a grove of laurels. I watched my sisters stretch their
    limbs
to finger pillars of light. They swayed and whispered together,
their leaves like tongues, green with envy, guessing at your name.

"Mother," they sighed, "we ran from temptation. We prayed to
    Father,
but our toes dipped into the warm, wet world; our fingers burst
with wild buds. Is this purity, Mother? Is this virtue?"

I knelt at their feet and wreathed their questions into my hair.
I tried to speak, but only coughed a thick darkness until it covered
    me,
until my brothers, satyr-faced and ashamed, peeked from their
    hiding places.

When it was safe, they sang of beauty—your beauty—which they
    could not see.
They danced, ecstatic and oedipal, tearing at their eyes for blindness.
"Mother," they sang, "we were lost in the woods.

When we prayed to Father, he separated us from the sheep,
left us for the stray Lamb. Remember your goat-headed boys,
    Mother,
seething in your milk." The song stopped short and they scattered.

It was not moonlight when it fell. It was not moonlight when it
    rested upon me.
It was clarity, warm and wise, when it circled me. And I saw you.
    And I saw
myself in you, kicking in a womb of glory, waiting to be born again.

[2014]

Missing Her

I think of her in a place of dreaming
I want her story, I want an end to the long search for her
I want her theology—to abandon the study of soft tracks and partial
prints for fullness

Touch my throat, the lack of her hard to swallow
Touch my eyes, tears of angry indignation at inequality
Touch my hands, molding them from fists into open palms ready to
receive her
Touch my neck and shoulders, bearing the burden of missing her

Could I see the curve of her wrist, her shapely fingers?
As Jared once saw the holy finger touching the clear stones
I offer the stone of my heart to her touch

[2014]

Small Gifts

Is your name hidden in the color of vermillion sandstone in this canyon
Is your voice in the trill of Canyon Wren or the call of Gambel Quail
Is your touch the silk of cottontail fur and soft desert breeze
Is your scent the delicious mixture of Sage, Pinyon and Juniper

Are you whispering a greeting like that of my bay gelding—a low
    soft nicker.
Is your love like the liquid brown of my dog's eyes as she gazes at me
from her comfort spot in the sun and thumps her tail
Is your light the scattered beauty of spring sun filtered through new
green leaves of a cottonwood tree

Do you sit by me on this solitary ledge—are your fingers the soft
brushing of Ponderosa needles on my hair and scalp
Did you offer me this display of clouds and sunrise so spectacular that
tears stream spontaneously from my eyes
Did you show me the curious red fox hunting gophers in my yard
Did you give me the glimpse of the greybrown lynx as I came early to
the pasture

Is your heart so big and wide, its chambers so miraculous and well
muscled that it can contain love and compassion big enough to surpass
all the human, animal and plant suffering that weighs on me
Will you sanctify my search for you with these continued small gifts
I will keep all these things in my heart and remember them

[2014]

First Time (Heavenly) Mother

Does Heavenly Mother know
what it is like to lock yourself
in the bathroom,
turn on the water, and cry
while the baby has colic?

Did she feel the aching pressure
of plugged milk ducts
or the nausea that comes
from the fifth night
with only three hours of sleep?

Does she remember the scent
of breastmilk souring in baby neck-folds?

After millennia of child bearing,
and filling world upon world
with her progeny,
does she remember her first few weeks
of motherhood?

And if she does,
could I take this moment while
my first child naps
to ask her a few questions?

[2015]

I Can't Imagine Her

Here on earth where we and myth exist
I cannot call you by a mortal name.
The sexist clichés (all we know) persist.

You stand beside our Father, co-exist,
yet never speak. A meek and modest flame
you seem to us, where we and myth exist.

I cannot fathom you as soloist.
Your part's a cameo. You have no fame
on earth where human symbols must persist.

Is there a spirit word for publicist?
I need to know an office you can claim
here on earth where we and myth exist.

I want to grasp you as a specialist.
I need new words. The ones I know lie tame
among the hard clichés that yet persist.

[2015]

My Mother (who is in Heaven)
Meets Heavenly Mother

I picture my mother (of seven) patiently standing
in a meandering, sluggish line
(women in one; men in another)
wondering in whispers
what happens next,
their gendered bodies wearing the earth's salt.

I picture (all of them) shifting their feet
in the surround of eager blue
circled by bulbous clouds, a foaming moon,
the blue and white the only absolutes.

Both lines finally thin
to zigzag through what look like Styrofoam church pews:
their inexact shapes (also) floating weightlessly.

Suddenly (but slowly, reverently) the women and the men
see advancing light
and know to bow and remove their soft-soled shoes.

I see my mother meet (for the first time)
her (our) Heavenly Mother
as the women's line tapers to the left
where She stands robed in flowing white,
her face ravishing and wise.

I see Her touch my mother's hand and lead her
toward a road widening to completion.

I see a multitude
of lone and dreary artifacts and trappings
tumbling through the atmosphere:

mix ing bowl and
dinner plate *frag* ments

                    melting metal forks
            and pans

Irons and vacuum cleaners.

                                    I see scraps
            jul ien nes

            dices peelings

                            floor and toilet rags

threads
            brushes

            recipe and diaper shreds

                            f e a t h e r s

bottle caps ...

I see the men, too, (open-mouthed),
          their own burdens giving way:

                    the strangling ties

                              the broken hammers, crooked nails

                    scarred briefcases

                              crumpled documents

their confident pulpits
now s p l i n t e r e d wood ...

I see the dos and don'ts,
the musts, ought nots, and nevers

deconstruct before my eyes:

First, into paragraphs,
               then to phrases,
                         then to words.

I see the sure and faithful lessons of the world
transcend the dots of end stops and conclusions.
I see them peter out to hills of soot.

I see our Mother's sweeping arm
wipe away their lusterless dust, leaving just
the blue and white (the only absolutes).

[2015]

Mother God

If you need me
to appear in a well-appointed cave
in the highest mountain,
where else would I be?

Here, a place for you under this white
robe. Here, asparagus and baby
artichokes.

What about the spirit
don't you understand? You are safe,
you are welcome.

Do you smell the raspberry cobbler
baking for your supper? Nourishment
to fill you, feed you, dissolve
the cataracts scaling your eyes.

Ah, my bluebells begin to open.

Listen ... the pure ring of glaciers
as they crack ... a fracture
begun in the smallest molecules
and the whole vast delusion
of my absence crashes into the sea,
salt-stung, bobbing off.

O my daughters, my sons, how often
would I have gathered you as an eagle
feeds her fledglings.
Take this into your throats:
rabbit of humility, salmon of desire,
snake of luminosity, of sight.

What about the feminine
present subjunctive eludes you—
that she be eternal? that she be
omnipotent? that she be wise?

[2015]

The Voice of God

is the voice I try for in poem after poem:
Mother of all omnipotence, Father of all
fathering. Because authorities
are always saying we should listen
to God and he will tell me what God wants, no
requires, you to do. Say the Kaddish. Cover her hair
with a sheitel. I am not Jewish and I'm hiding
within slipping pronouns and a faith
I know little about. For instance, in Judaic
thought, is there a hell? Outer darkness
it's called in Mormon thought, so far off
that only those close enough to feel
God's breath and still oppose His plans
will be lost in black-hole static.
There, that voice—do I not speak for God?
Which I can do on many topics,
although I can't, in print or church, say,
I believe in Mother and Father
who together created the universe,
who share all power and hope
to assign it to women as well as men on earth
as it is in heaven, as those who tell us
what to think might weave my words
into an eel trap and school me
into the shallows. Like all creatures,

I am meant to swim the depths,
the uninhibited oceans, where I can see
all the way to the cosmos and follow
the light back.

[2015]

Heavenly Mother Ode

She sits perched
on an invisible

throne. We are told

not to pray to her,
only to honor her

in remembrances

the same way we
think about the three

Marys. Can't we

stop taking it all
so literally—enough

splinters and nails

from the True Cross
in reliquaries all

over the world

to build an ark
for all the critters

to walk two by two

up the gangplank
and into the hold

where they'll all

eat and shit and
well, you know,

be fruitful and

multiply which is
why it's okay

to contemplate

the other half
of something else

no one has seen.

[2015]

A Parable

Why is there no mention
of Heavenly Mother

in the Standard Works

I once asked my Mission
President's wife, *not*

even in the Topical Guide,

and she glanced over
at her husband, deferring

to him. "Oh Elder Liu!,

why concern yourself
with mysteries we are

told not to contemplate

till the Hereafter?" By that
I wondered if he meant

after my mission or

after the real Hereafter
so I had to ask again

during one of our reunions

after General Conference
outside the Tabernacle

and with some bemused

exasperation he said, "Well,
maybe Heavenly Father

keeps her out of sight

so no one can take her
name in vain, something

like that." This was months

before a cop cruiser in
Ogden pulled up on his

parked car and took him

and his whore downtown
to get fingerprints taken—

their mugshots snapped.

[2015]

Strait is the Gate

Exactly how many
wives does my

Heavenly Father

have is a reasonable
question to ask

considering I was

made in His image
though it's not clear

why He has to be

white when some say
the historic Jesus

was black, the original

Christians actually
"Middle Eastern" people

of color, never mind

Constantine or Pope
Alexander VI who had

every icon of the Negro

Christ destroyed while
Cesare Borgia posed

for his lover Leonardo—

the same image a boy
named Joseph would gaze

upon centuries later

as he knelt in that grove
in Upstate New York,

not knowing he had

only 24 years to live.
Did Heavenly Mother

grieve as the Marys did

at the foot of that cross
soaked in blood? Did

She wince as Joseph's

arms shot straight up
to Heaven when the mob

who'd gathered outside

of that Carthage jail
let the bullets fly? How

could we not imagine

otherwise—Emma
rejecting the New

and Everlasting

Covenant to the end
of her days, demanding

to be the One and Only.

[2015]

This is Not a Prayer

Mom, can we talk? I promise
No amens, bent knees or hand clasping to blaspheme you.
Only me, just asking—

When did the title "Heavenly" take you so far away?

I ask Father sometimes, but the world is louder than
My little heart and divine echoes fade when I am told
A good girl would cover her ears and mouth.

When will "shh" become "She?"

[2015]

To the Unknown Goddess

When Paul stood on Mars' Hill,
He banished the superstition steeping
The altar TO THE UNKNOWN GOD.
In confidence, the apostle proclaimed,
"Whom therefore ye ignorantly worship,
Him declare I unto you."

Father! Unbound by the weak mirrors
Of men's idols, templed in no stone but heart,
Maker, mover and heavenly hand in all
That spins light from Pleiades to particle.
Poet and prophet have named Him
Through every age and traced His face.

Now, I wait for the one who will
Name Her, too—a mystery of mother
I am forbidden to send my prayers,
A woman rendered void and formless
Behind a veil of silence as a starless
Universe waiting to be dreamt into Being.

Yet, she has *always* gleamed beside God,
Faceting our souls with the gemmed rays
Of that teaspoon of astral dust we share
With the first massive stars that seeded
Every galaxy with new elements for suns.
No hush of dark dims Her ember-flare within.

[2015]

Utter it even to the end of the earth

Do not ask, "Woman, why weepest thou?"
I am as a wonder unto many, even I only,
I sit a queen lost in the wilderness of men's hearts.
I will speak in the anguish of my spirit:

Some say, "Our glorious Mother, calling her
By name her magnificence should be destroyed.
Put ashes on her head, put her away, let her alone;
The elect lady—why trouble ye her?"
As if to reverence me.

Would that my speech shall distill as the dew!
Ye cannot know of things which ye do not speak.
Know my name, search me ... know my heart:
Try me, and know my thoughts.

Do not ask, "But who are ye?
I AM that which is star, and the shadow of it
I AM the moon walking in brightness
I AM the burning rays of the rising sun.
I bare you upon the wings of the wind

Night and day with tears, honey in abundance,
A mist from the earth, and clear shining after rain.
I wish from the inmost part of my heart that
My voice shall sing in the windows again,

My love be with you all. Are you ready to hear me?
I will not keep silence—
The time of the singing of birds is come.
Behold, thy mother! Even from the beginning.
Set me as a seal upon thine heart.

[2015]

Octave

On the eighth day, Mother said:
Music will be your name, and you
will live among them—wretch

commoner, king—and speak unseen
to their loss, the petals of their joy,
their hollow pain. They will forget me,

but in your harmony may they hear
and in your turbulence recall
their origin and end, eternity and time

as womb. And if they shun you,
or extract the echo of my voice,
abuse you, or dismember the mystery

you are, that hell where no music is
will be their hole, where harp is plucked
and trumpet blown without a sound,

the drum as mute as the moon,
and cymbals as the stars before the sun.
But those who love you, I will love,

and though their hearts are rent
from birth to birth, your warm washing
and anointing oil will soothe the sorest

lifespan in an instant and deliver
the broken to their beginning: myself,
the Mother, expectant, staring at the fire.

[2015]

A Theology of Flesh

The part that caught my attention
was when she
cut off her breast
and carried it across the room
in a sterile tray
held out in front.

"My breast is not my
Femininity," she says.

Is that what frightens you?
Is that what darkens the glass?
Is it a breast—
a mass of tissue
and ducts
and lact—
that seems so foreign?

Take it, then!
Cut it off!
She will not die,
even breastless!

Is there another part of Her body that you find difficult?

Cut that off too! Take
hips
womb
lips
waist
calves
and buttocks!

Tie feathering tubes and
scoop smooth ovaries!

And when you have finished
and She reclines,
carved,
you will see
Her femininity intact.
But you should know
before you begin,

That my Mother's body is not the enemy.
And that my Goddess does not live
in order to make you comfortable
even though you may have heard otherwise.

She is a goddess—
familiar hearthfire flaring harsh.
Put down your knife.
Hush now.

Listen.

[2015]

In Her Hands

My sister slows entering the I-205,
rolls down the driver's side window,
stretches out her hand
holding two dollars for the man
holding a sign:
John 3:16—Anything Helps

In the train station parking lot,
I check my mascara in the visor mirror.
Across the street a woman rolls out
a sleeping bag in the doorway of a defunct building.
Who's hand is stretched out to her?
For God so loved the world ...

"I can't be God,"
I say to my sister.
Just the touch of the tiny bones in the hand
of my daughter fills me to the chest.
Even the giving of her babyhood to her own childhood
isn't a sacrifice I would trust myself to make.

People patterned with the same bones rest theirs
on ramps and in corners.
"But I want to be a mother, and I am,"
I say to my sister.
Is the palm of my own hand in the heart
of Heavenly Mother's love?

Is the ache of it the beginning of her glory?

[2015]

I Looked for Her

In mountain places and on sere plateaus, I looked for her.
Ascetics from their caves had fled those heights. I looked for her.

On windswept beaches of a palm-fringed bay, I looked for her.
In surging tides, I feared for paradise. I looked for her.

In line at food banks that ran out of food, I looked for her.
I'd lost my job and failed at rolling dice. I looked for her.

In homeless camps along old rail tracks, I looked for her.
Few blankets there; rain drizzled through the night. I looked for her.

In boats of refugees, I took my place. I looked for her.
With grieving men, I sat to hear last rites. I looked for her.

[2016]

In the temple I put all my senses to work searching for Her. A painting on the wall depicting a woman holding a giggling child in the air above her. The chandelier in the celestial room with the flowers on the table below it. The scent of fresh laundry on my rented temple clothes, and I thought of all the women's hands gathering, washing, folding and distributing. I got tired and rested my chin on my chest while I sat quietly and felt that someone understood. I listened, and listened, and listened through the words that were spoken, through the racing thoughts of my own mind, through my questions; I listened and the quietness spoke back, a quietness that got louder and louder, until as I walked down the stairs back to the dressing room, the words pressed themselves into the palms of my hands and soft places of my heart—"Spread my name like wildfire." When I got to the dressing room, I stood looking at myself in the mirror, my eyes pretty and deep like a still lake beginning to ripple before rain, a strength in them I had never noticed before.

[2016]

Some Women
Whose Stories I Have Known
or Am Getting to Know

Patricia Christensen. Mary Elizabeth Monahan. Emma Smith. Minerva Teichert. Chieko Okazaki. Lucy Mack Smith. Anne Bradstreet. Elizabeth Bishop. Patty Bartlett Sessions. Eleanor Roosevelt. Belle Spafford. Emmeline B. Wells. Esther Peterson. Lola Bickmore. Beulah Larsen. Laurel Thatcher Ulrich. Claudia Bushman. Terry Tempest Williams. Alice Louise Reynolds. Esther Peterson. Eliza R. Snow. Aung San Suu Kyi. Dorothy Canfield. Emily Dickinson. Virginia Woolf. Marie Curie. Marie Tharp. Maya Angelou. Mother Teresa. Noor Inayat Khan. Rosa Parks. Annistacia Potter. Lydia Hurst. Emma Day. Qiu Jin. Rosalind Franklin. Ruby Bridges. Sojourner Truth. Wilma Rudolph. Annie Dillard. Marilynne Robinson. Joyce Carol Oates. Louisa Barnes Pratt. Harriet Tubman. Irena Sadler. Jane Goodall. Amy Hone. Sharon Meyers. Karen Jackson. Becky Angus. Shelly Norton. Rita Christensen. MarieAnne Hoiland. Sage Rabino. Bayley Goldsberry. Mary Ann Christensen. My Heavenly Mother. Myself.

[2016]

The Priestess

In the beginning was the Word,
and She was God.
She breathed, "Let there be light,"
and shattered absence
with conception.
All was born.
She looked upon the earth,
teeming with a network of life.
And it was good.

She, God the Mother,
evolved woman from a lesser specimen,
and shared Her priestesshood with Eve,
The Mother of All Living.
Eve chose the fruit of
knowledge and intelligence,
protected under providence.
The children of God were born when
she disobeyed the laws of Eden.
And it was good.

Eve's daughters grew as
authorized agents,
keepers of keys,
temples of life,
attributed to God, Herself,

to enable all goodness and flourishing.
Her daughters acted in Her name,
creating life,
each a member of a greater whole.
And it was good.

My female body swollen
with Her priestesshood,
as it was with Mother Eve.
Infinite life within my womb,
pregnant with exponential love,
overflowing with sentience,
I felt my own daughter in motion.
And it was good.

My daughter was born.
In her first breath,
she wailed for the Mother,
"I am lost. Thirsty and suffocating.
Where is She?"
Placing my breast in her mouth,
I whispered to my daughter,
"The Mother is here,
as plain as air.
She surrounds you.
Claim your birthright and
breathe Her in.
You are not lost."
And it was good.

The Mother awaits
Her daughters to claim their priestesshood,
to act in the name of the Creator,
to summon the sacrament of life.
It was passed from mother to daughter,
beginning with the Word.

And it was good.

[2016]

Infinite Cadenza

To honor her we don't mention her,
we are told, as she flits tangible as
clouds.

If Heavenly Father is the body
she is the
blood:
poured, passed, swallowed whole
in tiny white cups and passed on.

We pray for those
not in attendance.
Does this include her
or is she there,
chapeled,
a curtain adorning a view?

Wherever we are
she is what is
missing.

[2016]

Mute Bird

"The very birds are mute."
—William Shakespeare (from "Sonnet XCVII")

Heavenly Mother would surprise
you: she is not white at all but ebony, wing of
raven, eagle, crow. She is the midnight
watch, the gaping rack of grandma's last
rasp, the wolf's heart, the tree bark
blackened that will not fall. Can you hear her
now? Life is born of her, as if from a horn of
plenty. She is my twelve year old's first
menses, dusk darkening to fall, the unfurled
womb, the rock sought, flung, and just as soon
forgotten.

[2016]

BONNIE SHIFFLER-OLSEN
& TRISH HOPKINSON

Three atheists and a Mormon walk into a café

The Bloody Mary mix is running low and they don't serve decaf.
We consider the things we must live without.

The lull of morning dissipates as caffeine seeps in
and conversation swells to lift the heavy fog of last evening.

We settle on vegetarian hors d'oeuvres and turn topics, lost
loves, lost sleep, directionless paths and longing for eureka or
    salvaged salvation.

We realize, we are all black sheep in our own right,
bleating and sheering our wool into soft piles on our laps.

From the discarded wolfishness we spin soft in-between spaces—
shared room, spooled experience, heathered aprons of human
    nature.

As the lunch rush clanks and rumbles we hardly take notice—
tuned in and pulled close, gathered like a sheaf of lamb's ear.

We enfold ourselves, unheard and unflustered by the bustling in-
    and-out crowd,
and culture our crooked necks in the attitude of attentive oblation.

If She does exist, at least one of us is certain She is listening
and can feel the warmth of Her breath as if we all just fell from her
 womb.

If She doesn't, knowing the shared breath of our awkward flock is
 enough
to call truth, and we go on braiding umbilical bonds to each other.

We inherit our ancient feminine divinity,
connected like a cat's cradle by the woolen threads of grace.

[2017]

Unspoken Prayer

My questions, pleas to you ascend unvoiced,
rendered slowly in the crunching of pine
needles under feet, sweepings of slippers
ascending spiral carpet stairs, fragile
turnings and siftings of tissue-papered
scripture sieved between verses. Do you speak
likewise, to me, in these wordless tongues?

Your husband's baritone servants sit, stand,
speak before lemon-oiled pulpits in black
suits, behind temple veils in snow-white ties,
while yours and you seem hidden, like naked
blushing skin under cotton-poly cloth.
In Eden, Elohim—a plural name—
commands creation from a single mouth.

This silence slices and divides, my God,
twists my heart into braided tourniquets.
Why don't you speak, stand, be seen beside him,
when he reveals himself? Why must bruises
blossom kneeling on hardwood floors, bed-side
half-God altars, lips forming prayers and praise
penned to off-white walls and just a portion

of the whole? My search for you is knotted
in the kneading and punching down of bowls
brimming with bread, in the reverent rustlings
of pleated robes slipping over shoulders,
in the clinking of plastic thimbles dropped,
empty of water, into trays. Command
me, Mother, to wash clean these muddied eyes

and tongue, for I long to taste your unearthed
fruits made tart by darkened loam, to drink your
sea of honeyed milk. Permit me, I pray,
some grasp of your skirts' hems, so I may walk
unburdened by this doubt—and forgive me
(oh God, forgive me) as I inch along
this cord dividing sacrilege and faith.

[2017]

ARTIST
STATEMENTS

LYNDE MOTT

A Mother's Love   TITLE PAGE

I would like to develop in our minds the reality of our
Heavenly Parents—more conspicuously, though, of our
Mother in Heaven.

Our doctrine in the LDS tradition holds the inviolate Truth
that the fullness of the Priesthood is only in a divine, sealed
pair. Or in other words, "God" is defined as an exalted man and
an exalted woman. Our Heavenly Father is not an eternal
bachelor.

I sense that the Divine Feminine has always been hidden in
plain view. Consider that an ancient symbol for the "mother
goddess" was a white dove. When the Savior was baptized, the
heavens opened, the Father's voice was heard, and perhaps
encapsulated in the Holy Ghost descending as a dove was also
the presence of our Mother's Spirit, further sanctifying and
witnessing to the work of Her son.

I wonder, further, if we may look forward to a day when we
will come before the Father with our brother and Savior at our

right and our Mother at our left, both in perfectly balanced roles of intermediaries and advocates before God on our behalf.

Here in this life, meanwhile, we are coming to the enlightened understanding that, on their own, both patriarchy and matriarchy are perversions. Only in genuine partnership will we embrace all of our humanity and opportunities. In partnership we will transcend the apparent paradoxes of strength and sensitivity, destruction and healing, separating and binding.

The decoupage in the background of the painting further delineates the variety of feminine roles through time, all of which our Heavenly Mother balances perfectly, including: solidarity and cooperation, demure and vivacious, heroic justice and tender mercy.

Instead of a gaudy, worldly bejeweled crown She wears an ancient symbol for free-flowing love—pink roses. The transition from patriarchy to partnership will only come about through a cleansing bath of love unfeigned and genuine forgiveness.

Mother has been weaving the threads of Her own chrysalis for generations. Now She will lift this veil of protection—not oppression—to emerge into full expression.

Those who have eyes to see will see Her. The time is right and ripe for us to see that She has always been with us. She will move from elusive to definite as She comes forth to train us to have the courage to create "the peaceable things of the Kingdom, bright as the sun, clear as the moon."

Springing Up

Springing Up was inspired by the passages in Alma 32 about our how we develop faith. When we try living by the word of God and plant the seed of faith in our hearts, our knowledge becomes "perfect in that thing, and [our] faith is dormant; and this because [we] know, for ye know that the word hath swelled your souls, and ye also know that it hath sprouted up, that your understanding doth begin to be enlightened, and your mind doth begin to expand."

While the figure standing behind the kneeling woman was originally designed as a representation of the spirit of revelation (being made up of words of scripture), many have connected with the figure as a representation of our Heavenly Mother. I feel this interpretation is equally valid, as our Heavenly Mother also watches over us as we develop and grow spiritually. It is gratifying to see people make and find different connections with this piece.

Breath of Life   PART ONE

The first chapter of Genesis states, "So God created man in his own image, in the image of God created he him; male and female created he them." In this painting I depicted Adam as he is created from the dust, by both a Heavenly Father and Heavenly Mother. Together they create and give the breath of life.

Virgin of the Mountain   PART TWO

I believe that the inspiration for this painting came from deep
recesses of my childhood's heart. I prayed in my bed every
night to see our Heavenly Mother. I imagined Her appearing
above me so fervently that, in the end, I decided that She had
indeed come. Many years later when I had reached my
maturity, that hope must have still hovered in my subconscious
because this painting seemed to have just used my hand to paint
itself. The sky and the crown presented themselves for obvious
reasons; I chose the mountain range to evoke the world below,
because my mind had evolved enough to encompass all of earth
in my prayers for divine love and protection.

In all my paintings, I start my creative process by visualizing an
image that I organize on the canvas by drawing the outlines of it
with brush and paint. From there, I will mix mostly cadmium
colors to create the myriad hues that I apply in bold, fresh
marks—intent on building pictures that express the vulnerability,
mystery, and delight of life on earth. I aim for beauty, truth,
order, focusing on enchantment rather than self-expression. My
compositions depict people, animals, and scenes as metaphors for
a particular state of being—the silence of an emotion, the portent
of a moment, or the spirit of a place. My work unwittingly draws
from the powerful sensations and visual excitement of my
childhood when people seemed magically connected to their
surroundings and to some invisible yet palpable realm.

Goddess Mother

It wasn't until I became a mother that I began to question my role in the church. Suddenly all I could see was a patriarchy appropriating the language of motherhood for its own benefit while categorically denying equal partnership and autonomy to women. I spent several years artistically exploring the themes of Heavenly Mother, both in and out of Mormon theology. Trying to find my fit, my own place. It was empowering and eye opening and also just a part of a longer journey that ultimately took me into a wider world of artistic endeavors.

Compression COVER

Tension is an important theme in Denise's work. Tension between flowing, organic forms, and rigid, geometric patterns. Tension between foreground and background. Tension between divinity and mortality, order and chaos, reality and dreams. These components are merely tools to express her phenomenological experiences and spiritual perceptions of the world around her. Her work begs the question, "Can one impart the beautiful richness and fleeting nuance of a phenomenological or spiritual experience to another through a static visual medium?" Above all else, it is the divine pursuit of beauty that drives her forward and compels her to create.

ENDNOTES

William W. Phelps
"A Song of Zion"

"A Song of Zion" was published in February 1844. This
is important to note because the poem's reference to a
"queen of heaven" shows that belief in Heavenly Mother
was espoused prior to Joseph Smith's death. Joseph
Smith was editor of the Times and Seasons newspaper
where the poem was published.

"the oil on Aaron": See Psalm 133:2.

"And Cassia from the east": See Psalm 45:8. Cassia was
one of the principal spices mixed with oil for anointing
priests, kings, and their garments. Likewise, the
coming King Messiah's robes will smell of cassia. Cassia
is not frequently used today, but was apparently a
highly valued commodity in biblical times. The root
word from which "cassia" derives in both Hebrew and
Arabic, *kiddah*, signifies a strip and refers to the strips of
bark from which the spice is made. In the spiritual
sense, cassia speaks of devotion (being stripped of
pride) and consecration (set apart) with a servant's
heart.

"'Tis like the dew of Hermon": See Psalm 133:3. Dew is a symbol for what is refreshing, quickening, and invigorating. Phelps, like the Psalmist before him, compares the influence of communal unity upon the church to the effect of dew upon vegetation.

"in his sermon": This seems to refer to the Council in Heaven in Abraham 3:22–28, a book Phelps had worked on translating with Joseph Smith.

"'Tis like a little leaven / The woman hid for good": See Matthew 13:33. Phelps' reference to this parable seems clear. The Queen of Heaven in this stanza did a similar act to the woman in Jesus' parable, hiding leaven (Christ) for the good of all, transforming and leavening the whole loaf of humanity through the gift of Her Son. See also Revelation 12.

"queen of heaven": See Psalm 45:9. This is not the queen of heaven referenced in Jeremiah 7:18.

"'Tis like the court of Zion, / Where garments all are white": See Revelation 3:4–5.

"like Judah's Lion": See Revelation 5:5.

"They'll eat the hidden manna, / Receive the precious stone": See Revelation 12:17; Doctrine & Covenants 130:9–11.

"And sing the great hosanna / Where God and Christ are one": See Revelation 7:9–10.

William W. Phelps
"A Voice from the Prophet: Come to Me"

This hymn was sung at the dedication of the Seventies Hall in Nauvoo, Illinois, in December 1844. Phelps described Joseph Smith introducing the saints to a mother in heaven, the queen, when they entered the celestial kingdom. This poem was actually a reworking of an earlier poem, "Vade Mecum" (or "Go with Me"), which Phelps wrote in January 1843 to Smith and was published in the August 1843 *Millennial Star*. In his reworking of the poem, Phelps added four new stanzas to the poem, including the one mentioning Heavenly Mother. But to call this simply a reworking would be a mistake. "Vade mecum" is an invitation from Phelps to Joseph Smith to have the prophet explore the celestial realm with him. Smith accepts Phelps' invitation in "The Vision" (possibly also written by Phelps), a poetic retelling of Doctrine and Covenants section 76, which details the three degrees of heavenly glory. The long poem offers language that opens portals to the unseen world, the original scripture providing the medium of revelation. "A Voice from the Prophet: Come to Me" concludes the exchange begun in "Vade Mecum" and continued in "The Vision." The prophet, now dead, invites Phelps (and the saints) to join him in the actual realm he once introduced via textual revelation. This is a powerful message for the saints only months after the prophet's death. Joel H. Johnson continued the dialogue with Phelps' poetry in his own "I'll Come to Thee, Joseph," accepting Joseph Smith's invitation in "A Voice."

"Where a heart can't conceive, nor a nat'ral eye see, / What the Lord has prepar'd for the just": See 1 Corinthians 2:9.

"Death, the wages of sin": See Romans 6:23.

"the knowledge that was, or that is, or will be": See Doctrine & Covenants 93:24.

"here's the myst'ry that man hath not seen": See Matthew 13:11–13.

"Here is Alpha, Omega, the first and the last": See Revelation 21:6.

"the Tree": See Revelation 2:7; 22:1–2.

Eliza R. Snow
"Invocation, or the Eternal Father and Mother"

While this hymn is commonly referred to as "O My Father," Snow originally titled it "My Father in Heaven." When she republished the poem as the first entry in her first volume of poetry, she renamed it

"Invocation, or the Eternal Father and Mother." We have opted to use the title Snow herself settled on for the poem. See Eliza R. Snow, "My Father in Heaven," *Times and Seasons*, vol. 6, no. 16, 15 November 1845, p. 1039; Snow, "Invocation, or the Eternal Father and Mother," *Poems, Religious, Historical, and Political*, vol. 1, Latter-day Saints' Book Depot, 1856, pp. 1–2.

"the key of knowledge": See Doctrine & Covenants 84:19; also Luke 11:53 in the Joseph Smith Translation of the Bible. The key is held by the Melchizedek priesthood.

Eliza R. Snow
"Excerpt from "To Mrs. [Sylvia Sessions] Lyon" (Trail Diary Version)"

This trail diary version differs from the published version.

John Lyon
"Epistle—Inscribed to S. R. [Sarah Richards]"

"Where Kings and Priests immortal bloom": See Revelation 1:6; 5:10.

"Who kept their first abode": See Abraham 3:26; Jude 1:6.

Jabez Woodard
    "Our Existence—Past, Present, and Future"

> This poem was published with the suggestion that it be
> sung to the "May Day" tune, possibly referring to J.
> Chadwick, "May-Day in England, Written to a
> celebrated Caledonian Air, as a Song or Glee, with
> Symphonies & Accompaniments," Firth & Hall (New
> York), 1840.

Orson F. Whitney
    "What is Life?"

> "Its clanking fetters claim as music, / Its darkness
> worship as 'twere light": See Isaiah 5:20.

> "Their dream: 'To-day; there comes no morrow'": See
> Isaiah 22:13; 1 Corinthians 15:32; Luke 12:19.

> "Did morning stars hymn loud hosannas": See Job 38:7.

> "My home is where the starry kingdoms / Roll round
> the Kingdom of the Sun!": See Abraham 3.

Orson F. Whitney
    Excerpts from Elias: An Epic of the Ages

> The excerpts we have included were culled from the
> 1904 edition published by The Knickerbocker Press

(New York) and freely accessible online via Google Books. See pp. 11, 42, 100, 103.

"Queen of the future, Eve of coming worlds, / Mother of sun-born myriads yet to be": See Doctrine & Covenants 132:20–24.

"Spirit and body, blending, make the soul": See Doctrine & Covenants 88:15.

"That heirs with Christ may reign as queens and kings / Where endless union endless increase brings": See Doctrine & Covenants 132:20–24.

"And restitution's edict seal and bind / Eternal matter to eternal mind": Doctrine & Covenants 93:33–35.

"No man without the woman in the Lord": See 1 Corinthians 11:11.

J. H. Ward
"To Unseen Friends"

"Ere we left golden portals": See Doctrine & Covenants 137:2.

Alfred Osmond
Excerpt from "Thoughts on Death"

"May not, through sin, break those endearing ties / That bind man to his God and chain the earth and

skies": Osmond alludes to the dual applications of the
sealing power: 1) the power to seal humans into family
units, making them links in a chain all of the way back
to Adam and Heavenly Parents; 2) the power to seal the
heavens from the earth, restraining rains from falling.

Maxine Hanks
"Truth Eternal"

The title is taken from Eliza R. Snow's "Invocation, or
the Eternal Father and Mother": "Truth is reason—
truth eternal / Tells me I've a mother there" (lines 23–
24).

"in the memory of mothers and daughters of light":
Inspired by Carol Lynn Pearson's *Daughters of Light*
(1973). Written after hearing Carol Lynn speak at
Ricks College in 1976.

The French Linguistic Committee of the Church of Jesus Christ of Latter-day Saints
"Souviens-toi, mon enfant"

*Cantiques de l'Église de Jésus-Christ des Saints des Derniers
Jours*. Church of Jesus Christ of Latter-day Saints, 1993,
no. 179. Used with permission.

This translation was assisted by examining translations
by Rixa Freeze, Linda Peterson, and J. Alexander
Curtis. For an explorative translation that takes more

artistic liberties, we recommend Lisa Bolin Hawkins'
"Remember, My Child": sisterlykindness.com/2017/
08/16/remember-my-child-souviens-toi/.

Simon Peter Eggertsen
"On the Mountain Road to Taos"

Influenced by a viewing of Georgia O'Keeffe's *Black
Mesa Landscape/Out Back of Marie II*, 1930, and *Sky Above
the Clouds*, 1962–63 (Georgia O'Keeffe Museum, Santa
Fe, New Mexico).

Maxine Hanks
"Here the Whole Time"

"You reappeared in glimpses, 'a movement and a rest'":
The Gospel of Thomas, 50: "If they ask you: What is
the sign of your Father in you?, say to them: It is a
movement and a rest." [Brill transl.]

Steven L. Peck
"My Turn on Earth"

As published in Peck's novel-disguised-as-master's-
thesis, *Gilda Trillim: Shepherdess of Rats*, the poem
appears under the title "Vignette 11: Gilda's Poem My
Turn on Earth. Written Circa 1951." The novel also
offers this introduction to the poem: "The following
theological poem was found in one of Trillim's high

school notebooks. While the title appears to be tongue-in-cheek, playing off of the Lex De Azevedo and Carol Lynn Pearson LDS musical *My Turn on Earth: A Family Musical Play* from the 1970s, and added years after she wrote this, the rest seems a kind of poetic theology. What is astonishing is that she seems to anticipate many current issues—like unscientific intelligent design creationism.

"There is much informal discussion among Trillim scholars about what this work was supposed to be. It seems to be a play of sorts. Or perhaps a hymn of praise. It is clearly a poem and she draws on several poetic forms in its construction: sonnet, villanelle, sestina, pantoun [sic], free verse, and even limerick. It is difficult to classify and lies outside the genre Trillim usually uses in her minimalist novels" (p. 99).

Rachel Hunt Steenblik
"What Rosemary Taught Me"

Rosemary Radford Ruether. *Sexism and God-talk: Toward a Feminist Theology*. Beacon Press, 1993.

S.E. Page
"Utter it even to the end of the earth"

A found poem. "Found poetry" incorporates words, phrases, and lines from other sources—in this case, the scriptures—in order to give them new meaning. The

following is a list of scriptural references in the order
that they appear in the poem: Isaiah 48:20; D&C 8:10;
John 20:15; Psalms 71:7; 1 Kings 18:22; Revelation
18:7; Mosiah 23:30; Job 39:28; D&C 88:91; Job 7:11;
Matthew 16:14; D&C 138:39; D&C 20:73; D&C
20:73; Acts 19:27; 2 Samuel 13:19; Deuteronomy
22:29; John 12:7; 2 John 1:1; Mark 14:6; Alma 47:22;
D&C 50:43; Matthew 7:12; Deuteronomy 32:2; Alma
30:15; Ephesians 6:20; Isaiah 52:6; Psalms 139:23;
D&C 8:10; Acts 19:15; Exodus 3:14; Abraham 3:13;
Job 10:21; 2 Kings 20:10; Exodus 3:14; Job 31:26;
Exodus 3:14; D&C 121:11; Exodus 19:4; 2 Samuel
22:11; Acts 20:31; 1 Nephi 18:6; Genesis 2:6; 2
Samuel 23:4; Alma 13:27; John 17:21; Psalms 142:1;
Zephaniah 2:14; Psalms 71:20; 1 Corinthians 16:24;
D&C 34:4; Luke 22:33; Psalms 17:6; Isaiah 65:6; Song
of Solomon 2:12; Matthew 12:47; Abraham 1:3; Song
of Solomon 8:6.

NOTES ON HISTORICAL FIGURES

The short biographies in this section offer details about the lives of the early Mormon figures whose work we've featured in Part One: 1844–1910.

WILLIAM H. [HENRY] APPERLEY was born in Duncannon, Ireland, in 1845. Apperley's father, William, served with the Royal Marines in India. While away on duty, his wife, Sarah Meaton, converted to Mormonism, and William joined the church upon his return. In 1855, when he was nine years old, Apperley immigrated to Utah with his family and crossed the plains with the Richard Ballantyne Company. When Apperley grew up, he worked as a professor in the newly-opened Brigham Young College in Logan, Utah, and married Lydia Mangreen, who bore him eight children over the course of ten years. Apperley's teaching responsibilities at this university were diverse. A college circular reported that he taught "Spanish, Book-keeping, Grammar, (Winter Course),

Book of Mormon Studies, Key to Theology, Orthography and Punctuation, English Classics, Ethics."

In 1881, Apperley left his wife and children at home while he served a mission in England. While on that mission, Apperley wrote an article for the *Millennial Star* that intended to use philosophy and reasoning to demonstrate the immortality of the soul. Apperley considered:

> If man, in his present state, could be told the mysteries of his spiritual birth and destiny, he would probably understand it as well as the prattling infant, when commencing to lisp its mother tongue, could understand the laws that gave him mortal birth. But reason and analogy enable us to come to the following conclusion: The elements that form the body could not receive an earthly birth without earthly parents; neither could the spirit receive its spiritual birth without spiritual parents. But as our earthly parents die and return to the dust, so we, in our turn, must lay our bodies in the silent grave, but as our spiritual parents are eternal and unchangeable beings, it follows that man will live and retain his identity while God lives and the universe exists.

When Apperley returned from his mission, he participated in the Logan Temple Lectures following the completion of that temple in 1884, giving a lecture on language and English literature, which was subsequently published. Unfortunately for Apperley, his time away in England had not been good on Lydia, who struggled with childrearing and having an absent husband. One day she ran off to San Francisco. Apperley followed and retrieved her, but she fled again upon her return. At this time he secured a divorce, and 7 of his children ended up scattered over Utah, with the exception of his daughter, Ida.

Apperley married Charlotte Ann Lamoreaux in 1908. Two years later, he expressed his philosophical ruminations on spiritual parentage in poetic form in a slim volume of poetry titled *A Souvenier*. We've included herein the more explicit references to Heavenly Mother from his poem "To My Fellow Workers," although Heavenly Parents are also referenced in "To President William Budge (On His Eightieth Birthday)." Apperley died in 1923 in Washington, Utah.

"To My Fellow Workers." *A Souvenier*. 1910.

"Destiny of Man." *The Latter-day Saints' Millennial Star*, vol. 44, no. 24, 1882, p. 373.

C. C. A. [CARL CHRISTIAN ANTON] CHRISTENSEN

was born in Copenhagen, Denmark, in 1831. He studied at the Royal Academy of Art in Copenhagen from 1847 to 1853, learning a gritty and realistic artistic style, which sought to preserve Danish culture against German expansionism. During his studies, in 1850, he converted to Mormonism. Three years later he served a mission to Denmark and Norway, after which he emigrated to America from Liverpool. Before crossing the Atlantic, he married Elsie Scheel Haarby aboard the *Westmoreland*. Following the overseas journey, they took the railroad to Iowa City and completed the rest of the trek to the Utah Territory by handcart.

Settling in Sanpete County, Christensen homesteaded in Mt. Pleasant, Fairview, and finally in Ephraim, struggling to put his professional training to use. To make ends meet, Christensen worked as a farmer, bricklayer, house painter, and even railroad worker. While working to support his family, he served two additional Scandinavian missions. Following the second, Christensen married Maren Petterson, engaging in the then common LDS practice of polygamy.

Eventually, Christensen found work suited to his aptitudes: painting murals in the St. George temple, the Manti temple, and the Ephraim tabernacle, and stage painting for a theater in Springville. He was also commissioned to create Bible and Book of Mormon paintings, some of which were used by the LDS Sunday School in classrooms. He is most famous for his 22 (originally 23) paintings of pre-Utah Mormon history (his "Mormon Panorama"). Painted over several years beginning in 1878, these large paintings (7 ft. x 10 ft.), begin with Joseph Smith's early religious experience in New York State and end with the Mormon pioneers' 1847 entry into the Salt Lake Valley. Christensen delivered Mormon history lectures with the paintings throughout the Mountain West states.

While he was primarily a painter, Christensen was also an accomplished writer. He translated LDS hymns into Danish and served as a reporter and later an editor for the *Bikuben*, Utah's Danish/Norwegian newspaper. During his third mission to Denmark from 1887 to 1889, he worked as the editor of the *Scandinaviens Stjerne*. In 1901 he began working in the LDS

Church Historical Department, compiling the history of the Scandinavian Mission.

Christensen also wrote Danish hymns and poetry. His contributions to the *Bikuben* brought Ephraim some fame, although Christensen did not think much of his writing: "They call me a poet," he recited at a Scandinavian festival in Logan in 1892, "but I'm only a painter, and Danish is my daily speech." He wrote many comic poems about Scandinavian life that elated the immigrant Mormon populace and he was proud of the Danish tongue, speculating that the Adamic language was a form of Scandinavian. Many of his poems mention a Heavenly Mother, including *"Vort Himmelhjem," "Nu er dit Tid,"* and *"Et aandeligt Lysbillede,"* the latter of which we've included in this collection.

> "Et aandeligt Lysbillede." *Poetiske Arbejder Artikler og Afhandlinger tilligemed hans Levnedsløb.* John S. Hansen, 1921.

WILLIAM C. [CHASE] HARRISON was born in London, England in 1852. His father, William, joined the Mormon church and took him and his siblings to America in 1856, abandoning their mother and traveling aboard the ship *Horizon*. In America, the older William worked as a tinner and was tarred and feathered in Philadelphia for his belief in Mormonism; he also married Hannah Adams and kept the family heading west, seeking work and escape from the American Civil War. In 1862, the family migrated across the plains to Utah with the James Wareham Company. After settling in the American West, the younger William married Mary Elizabeth Forsyth and lived a while in Lake Point, Utah; Emmett, Idaho; and Spanish Fork, Utah. Following Mary's passing in 1907, Harrison married Eunice Parker. He died in 1935 in Payson, Utah.

His poem "Our Mother in Heaven," is the most well-known of many works that riffed on and conversed with Eliza R. Snow's "Invocation." Harrison's poem was set to music in the *Juvenile Instructor*. The song left enough of an impression on other Mormons that it was recorded in journals and sung at some public gatherings.

"Companion Poem to Eliza R. Snow's 'Invocation.'"
The Juvenile Instructor, vol. 27, no. 5, 1892, p. 163.

JOHN LYON was a Utah pioneer who served as a missionary in England and wrote two collections of verse, *Harp of Zion* (1853) and *Songs of a Pioneer* (1923), each published posthumously by his son. Lyon was born in 1803 into a poor, illiterate family in Glasgow, Lanarkshire, Scotland. His father died when he was eight, and he had a poor relationship with his eventual step-father. He took apprenticeships as a weaver and cotton-spinner, and then studied at night schools to further his education, while enjoying the occasional bare-knuckle boxing fight. He worked as a newspaper man, a "penny-a-liner," gathering news and correspondence for local papers, and assisted in publishing poetry anthologies, while his wife, Janet, kept their children involved in the weaving business. Although he was illiterate until he turned 25, Lyon later wrote and published many poems. After joining the LDS church in 1844, he published 32 poems in the *Millennial Star* and came to be known as "The Scottish Bard." Seven of his poems became LDS hymns, although none remain in the current official LDS hymnal.

With some encouragement from Mormon leaders Orson Pratt and Franklin D. Richards, 105 of Lyon's poems were gathered in the *Harp of Zion*, the first Mormon collection of poetry. While Lyon's earlier work addressed socio-political reform, his later religious works were didactic (albeit some with a humorous tone), touching on LDS theology and seeking to uplift followers of the faith. Most of Lyon's poems explore, extol, and animate religious themes, such as fleeing Babylon, gathering to Zion, the Second Coming, assisting the poor, and praising specific leaders. He sold 2,000 copies of *Harp of Zion*, and donated the funds to the Perpetual Emigrating Fund to help saints reach the Utah Territory (referred to at the time as Zion).

After serving in missionary capacities in the British Isles, Lyon emigrated to Utah and there served as a territorial librarian and superintendent (secretary and recorder) of the Endowment House. He also wrote as a literary critic for *The Deseret News* and published 25 short stories and prose sketches in Utah territory periodicals like *The Mountaineer*, *Tullidge's Quarterly Magazine*, and *The Contributor*. Lyon maintained a friendly relationship with Eliza R. Snow and participated in intellectual circles that included Edward Tullidge, Karl G.

Maeser, and William S. Godbe. Lyon's posthumously published book, *Songs of a Pioneer*, collected poems associated with Utah. Lyon passed away in 1889.

"Epistle—Inscribed to S. R." *The Harp of Zion*. S. W. Richards, 1853, pp. 145–47.

ALFRED OSMOND was born in Willard, Utah, and grew up in Bear Lake County and southern Wyoming. This environment exposed him firsthand to work on the farm and the range. He studied at many universities, including the University of Utah, University of MichiganAnn Arbor, University of Chicago, Harvard, and Columbia. He was employed in Brigham Young University's English department for 28 years, teaching classes in literature and creative writing and serving as department chair. While juggling teaching responsibilities, advocating Shakespeare, and giving recitals, Osmond wrote verse. His poetry was published in Utah magazines and newspapers, as well as the *Journal of Education*. He published several books, including *The Exiles*, *My Philosophy of Life*, *Married Sweethearts*, *The Happy Humorist*, and *The Poetical Works of Alfred Osmond*, along with other collections of poetic verse.

Osmond's work often reflected on the subject of death; because of this, he was considered a pessimist, something about which he was very self-conscious. However, he felt that this mortal soberness was counterbalanced by his commitment to writing about Christian-Mormon doctrines; in this regard, he referenced Heavenly Mother. She appears, for instance, in his poem "Thoughts on Death" (which we've excerpted in this anthology), as well as in the first canto of "The World in Darkness." In this canto, Osmond notes how religion, which could comfort humanity (particularly as regards death), has fallen out of favor on the earth and returned to its heavenly source. Likewise, the Holy Ghost is grieved by human actions, and the gifts of the spirit have disappeared. Osmond explains that:

> An evidence that He was not with man—
> The Holy Ghost, the Holy King and Queen
> Had flown from earth; the Gospel's glorious plan
> Did not exist below, still on time's river ran.

The presence of the Gods—Father, Mother, Son, and Holy Ghost—and Their plan for man have all evaporated from human awareness.

"Thoughts on Death." *The Poetical Works of Alfred Osmond.* G. Q. Cannon & Sons, 1891, pp. 201–02.

"The World in Darkness." *The Poetical Works of Alfred Osmond.* G. Q. Cannon & Sons, 1891, p. 77.

WILLIAM W. [WINES] PHELPS was a writer, publisher, editor, scribe, educator, lawyer, judge, politician, and early LDS church leader. Born in 1792 to Enon Phelps and Mehitabel Goldsmith in Hanover, New Jersey, Phelps' family migrated to New York when he was a young man. Phelps received a common school education, but he taught himself many subjects. As an adult, he became a newspaper editor for the *Western Courier* and anti-Masonic periodicals *Lake Light* and the *Ontario Phoenix*. He also helped organize the Anti-Masonic party and hoped to become the party nominee for Lieutenant Governor of New York.

When the Book of Mormon was published by E. B. Grandin, Phelps purchased copies to sell and read the volume. Captivated by the text, he and his wife Sally moved to Kirtland, Ohio, to reside near the main body of the Latter-day Saints. After joining the LDS church, Phelps assisted with early church publications, at Joseph Smith's request, editing *The Evening and the Morning Star*, *Missouri Advertiser*, *Times and Seasons*, and *Nauvoo Neighbor*. In addition, Phelps helped compile and publish the Book of Commandments and the Doctrine and Covenants, and served as a scribe in Joseph Smith's translation of the Book of Abraham.

A prolific writer of hymns, Phelps assisted Emma Smith in compiling the church's first hymnal; he wrote 28 of the 90 hymns included in that compilation. Many of his hymns remain in the official LDS hymnal today, including the notable "The Spirit of God" (sung at LDS temple dedications), as well as "Gently Raise the Sacred Strain," "Praise to the Man," and "If You Could Hie to Kolob."

Phelps quickly moved up ecclesiastical ranks and served in various civil capacities for the LDS church. He served as a counselor to David Whitmer in the church's first stake, was a member of the Nauvoo City Council and the Council of Fifty, and served in the Utah territorial legislative assembly (1851–

57). He also served on the board of regents for the University of Deseret. He was excommunicated three times: first for profiting from Far West land deals and reneging on a temple donation, second for testifying against church leaders during the 1838 Richmond Hearings, and third for marrying two women without receiving proper authorization to practice plural marriage. These separations notwithstanding, he continuously repaired his ties with the church.

Phelps' writings include the first published account of Heavenly Mother. In February 1844, four months before the death of Joseph Smith, he published a poem known as "A Song of Zion" in the *Times and Seasons*, a periodical that Joseph Smith edited. In a messianic reading of Psalm 45:9, Phelps mentioned in this poem the "queen of heaven"; for Phelps, this was not the pagan entity mentioned in Jeremiah, but a female goddess present at the premortal selection of Jesus as the Christ in the Council in Heaven. While Phelps' "queen of heaven" was not initially described as Heavenly Mother, she quickly became so in later writings and poems. In a letter dated December 25, 1844, and published on January 1, 1845, Phelps chronicled the premortal scene for Joseph Smith's brother, William. His letter mentions Heavenly Mother, whom he refers to as the Queen of Heaven. Therein the Son of God is anointed for his calling on Earth and crowned in the midst of his brothers and sisters, while Heavenly Mother stands with approving virtue and smiles upon her Son, who kept the faith as the heir of all things. Phelps referred again to this scene in his *Deseret Almanac, for the Year of our Lord, 1853* and his *Deseret Almanac, for the Year of our Lord, 1854*.

In "If You Could Hie to Kolob" Phelps defends an infinitist position related to the origins of divinity. He asks readers to consider if, having the capacities of angelic beings, they could search and find "the generation where Gods began to be" or "view the last creation, where Gods and matter end"; Phelps' answer was no. Rather, he argues that the Spirit guides us to the contrary view—that "the works of Gods continue" and that there is "no end to [the divine] race [of Gods]." There is, as he describes in his work, "Ruth," an unending "sacred chain of [generative] being," of "ever-kin with kin."

"A Song of Zion." *Times and Seasons*, vol. 5, no. 3, 1844.

"A Voice from the Prophet: Come to Me." *Times and Seasons*, vol. 6, no. 1, 1845.

LOUISA "LULA" GREENE RICHARDS was born in 1849 in Kanesville, Iowa, during a cholera outbreak. Her family traveled to Salt Lake City in 1852 after Brigham Young ordered the evacuation of Kanesville with all of Pottawattamie County. Richards grew up in an educated household; her father was a teacher and served for a time as the mayor of Provo. At age 18, she and her sister, Lissa, opened a small school, but Lula was frustrated by her own impatience with the students as well as with her lack of formal education; so in 1869 she returned to school in Salt Lake City, where she honed her skill as a writer. Early poems she submitted to the *Salt Lake Herald* and *Deseret News* under the name "Lula" were well-received. As a great-niece of Brigham Young, she formed a close relationship with Eliza R. Snow, whose first poetry collection Richards helped bring about by selling advance subscriptions.

Richards' personal initiative and skill with the pen caught the attention of Edward Sloan, editor of the *Salt Lake Herald*; and in 1872 he selected her to be the editor of a new newspaper targeted at women: the *Woman's Exponent*. She was only 23 at the time and had little experience with journalism. Unsure of her qualifications for such a position and worried about making her career a priority when she was yet unmarried, she balked at Sloan's offer; he pressured her to accept by telling her that the periodical would probably be scrapped if she didn't step in. She accepted his offer only after Eliza R. Snow convinced her that it was a great duty to cultivate the minds of those already born, as it was to bring new life into the world, and on the condition that Brigham Young officially recognize the appointment. Young made it an official Church mission for her and set her apart for the calling. With her conditions met, Richards served as the periodical editor for the next five years. The scope for the paper was admittedly broad: "every subject interesting and valuable to women," things it sought to represent without stirring any conflict between men and women. In her editorials in subsequent issues of the *Exponent*, Richards argued for women's right to vote, obtain an equal education, choose their occupation, and freely practice their religion. The paper also reported local Relief Society news and published defenses of polygamy, which continued until the 1890 Manifesto.

As time passed, Emmeline B. Wells took a greater hand in the journal; and after five years' involvement with the periodical, Richards stepped down from her position, which passed to Wells. Unburdened of her editorial responsibilities, Richards began to focus more on her family. This was no surprise given that her two daughters had died in infancy and she may have felt that her work on the periodical took away time she should have given to them. Nonetheless, she wouldn't resign from her mission on the *Woman's Exponent* until she again received the consent of President Young. To him she noted that "In years to come, I hope to be prepared to enter again unto such labors, with renewed energies and increased capabilities."

Richards lived true to her words. She continued to write and edit as her family grew (she had seven children, only four of whom reached adulthood; all three of her daughters died). In 1883, she began work on the *Juvenile Instructor*, an LDS periodical edited by George Q. Cannon. She wrote and edited the column "Our Little Folks" until 1907. Her poems appeared in the *Woman's Exponent*, *Improvement Era*, *Young Woman's Journal*, *Children's Friend*, *Relief Society Magazine*, and *Juvenile Instructor*. Her own collection of poetry, *Branches That Run Over the Wall*, was published in 1904.

Richards' poetry on Heavenly Mother is not referenced often, and like other poems in this collection, has not received the historical attention that Eliza R. Snow's "Invocation, or the Eternal Father and Mother" has. Nonetheless, Richards' Heavenly Mother poems are striking in terms of their cohesion and narrative structure. For instance, "A Thread of Thought," written for the Relief Society Jubilee in 1892, portrays a loving Heavenly Mother who is deeply interested in the development of her daughters. In "A Welcome," the "kind word" humans use

to greet one another foreshadows the "loving welcome" we
may someday receive from Heavenly Father and Mother; this
greeting includes "Mother's kiss." And "Rest and Progression"
follows a deceased person's path through the afterlife, starting
at a funeral and moving on to this person's heavenly destiny,
where the veil of forgetfulness is rent and the person is
reunited with Heavenly Parents.

> "A Thread of Thought." *Branches that Run Over the Wall,
> a Book of Mormon Poem, and Other Writings.* Magazine
> Printing Company, 1904, pp. 191–93.

> "A Welcome." *Branches that Run Over the Wall, a Book of
> Mormon Poem, and Other Writings.* Magazine Printing
> Company, 1904, pp. 264–66.

CHARLES EDMUND RICHARDSON was born in
Manti, Utah, in 1858. He married two wives, Sarah Louisa
Adams and Sarah Rogers, and was called to serve a mission in
Colonia Diaz, Chihuahua, Mexico. Richardson served as the
Legal Advisor to—and later the only attorney for—the
Mormon colonists in Mexico and enrolled as a law student at
the University of Mexico to increase his capacity to serve that
group. His work required much travel between widely
scattered colonies and between municipal, state, and federal
courts. Besides his work in the courtroom, Richardson taught
day and night school for the colonists; operated a blacksmith
shop, shoe repair shop, and drugstore; and built a windmill,
grist mill, and canal. In the midst of these efforts, Richardson

found time for literary pursuits, which included translating the hymn "O My Father" into Spanish; his translation is still used in the LDS Church's Spanish hymnal. He also wrote his own poetry, publishing the long work *Footprints of Gospel Feet for the Modest-in-Heart* in 1891. Richardson wasn't satisfied with the book and tried to recall its publication, but did so too late.

Heavenly Mother features prominently in *Footprints of Gospel Feet*, where Richardson provides the most detailed portrayal of Her in Mormon narrative art, next to the ones offered in Laura Moench Jenkins' short story, "Beyond the Portals" (1916), or (much later) in Mahonri Stewart's play, *The Emperor Wolf* (2014). In 1925, Richardson published a hymn in the *Improvement Era* that features Heavenly Mother. In it, he calls saints to seek the highest degree of salvation:

> From sacrifice, then, shrink not
> A higher heav'n to own,
> Where Father, Mother, Brother
> Can share with you their throne;
> Where Gods shall be your helpers
> While angels do your will,
> Eternal progress guiding,
> The goal, perfection still.

Heavenly Mother is shown to be a ruling influence in heaven, possessing a throne which She shares with Father and Son (our Brother Christ) and can share further with all Her exalted children.

Footprints of Gospel Feet for the Modest-in-Heart. Cannon
Publishing House, 1891.

"Hymn." *Improvement Era*, vol. 18, 1925, p. 433.

ELIZA R. [ROXCY] SNOW SMITH was born in
Becket, Berkshire County, Massachusetts, in 1804 to Oliver
Snow and Rosetta L. Pettibone. Her parents were open-
minded Baptists and English descendants of what she described
as "genuine Puritan stock." While a toddler, her parents
migrated to the Western Reserve Valley in Mantua, Ohio.
Upon their arrival, her father established a good farm, built one
of Mantua's first permanent homes, and got involved in public
business as a town and county official. Eliza attended a local
grammar school and, when able, served as a secretary for her
father, who was a justice of the peace.

The Snows were a hospitable family and allowed people
from various religious persuasions to meet and converse in
their home. In 1828, Oliver and Rosetta joined Alexander
Campbell's Disciples of Christ, under the tutelage of Sidney
Rigdon. LDS missionaries frequented Mantua, and Joseph
Smith called at the Snow home in 1831. Oliver and Rosetta
converted to Mormonism soon thereafter, but Eliza took until
1835 to join them. Within a year, she had migrated to
Kirtland, Ohio, where she donated her inheritance towards the
construction of the Kirtland temple. She received a nice lot of
land for her donation and ran a school for girls while working
as a boarding governess to Joseph Smith's children.

Eliza followed the saints in their migrations to Adam-Ondi-Ahman, Missouri, and Nauvoo, Illinois, and witnessed firsthand the persecution and brutality that plagued early Mormons. She herself was reportedly gang-raped by eight Missourians during the 1838 Mormon War; the attack may have left her unable to bear children. In Nauvoo, she ran another school and secretly became a plural wife to Joseph Smith. She was also involved in creating the bylaws of the first Relief Society; as secretary of that organization, she took detailed notes of its purposes and proceedings.

After the Prophet's death, the Relief Society went defunct and Eliza married Brigham Young as a plural wife, crossing the plains with his household and arriving in the Salt Lake Valley in 1847. Her first decade in the valley involved recovering from illness; writing and compiling her poetry; and, with her brother Lorenzo (future President of the LDS Church), founding a Polysophical Society, a select group of intelligentsia. Channelling Eliza's skills into more practical matters, Brigham Young called her in 1855 to preside over the sisters' work in the newly dedicated Endowment House. Around a decade later, he called her to reestablish the Relief Society. Inspired by her call, she traveled throughout the Utah Territory, using her Nauvoo notes to guide her mission. She also served as President of the Relief Society until 1887.

During her presidency, she opened the Deseret Hospital, operated cooperative stores, promoted silk manufacture, and sent women for professional medical training. She was also the primary organizer for the Young Ladies' Mutual Improvement Association in 1870 and assisted Aurelia Spencer Rogers in establishing the Primary Association in 1878. Snow died in

1887 in Salt Lake City and was interred in the Brigham Young family cemetery.

Snow's work in the publishing world was vast and distinguished. She had poetry published (mostly on patriotic themes) in local Ohio newspapers from 1826 to 1832, and became famous and sought after by contemporary literary figures. Upon her conversion to Mormonism, her poetry graced both secular and Mormon periodicals and was set to music in LDS hymnals. This included her 1845 "My Father in Heaven," a poem written in the attic of Stephen Markham's home soon after her father (who had grown disaffected with the church) died in Walnut Grove, Illinois. She later renamed the poem "Invocation, or the Eternal Father and Mother," and placed it at the beginning of her first volume of poetry. It is best known to Mormons as the hymn "O My Father" and is the most popular Mormon poem/hymn noting belief in a Heavenly Mother. It is also widely (and erroneously) believed to be the first Mormon poem describing Mother; this honor, rather, goes to W. W. Phelps' "A Song of Zion."

Snow's poem is remarkable because it marks a shift in the dialogue about Heavenly Mother. Instead of focusing on the wonder of Her existence, or having Her stand at events like some trophy (as in some of Phelps' earlier poems), "Invocation" manifests a yearning to relate with Her and be in Her presence. The last stanza calls to both Heavenly Parents, sharing a desire to fulfill Their shared will: that which "[the Mother and Father] sent [her] forth to do." Snow hopes to return to Their presence with Their "mutual approbation," not just the Father's.

When set to music, the poem became immensely popular. It was the favorite hymn of several Church leaders, including Brigham Young, and was sung at Snow's funeral. It also appears on a monument near her grave. The hymn's popularity spawned a series of imitative works by other LDS poets. For instance, J. Urban Allred recorded in his journal in 1899 that a Ms. Edwards, of the Willard Ward Sunday School, sang a song she had composed, which was a clear reworking of Snow's poem. This imitative effort also manifests in William C. Harrison's "Our Mother in Heaven" (1892) (included in this anthology), which Harrison appropriately describes as a "companion hymn" to "O My Father." Harrison's poem parallels the transition in "O My Father" from premortal to mortal to postmortal life, and addresses Heavenly Mother throughout those stages. Another example of indebtedness to Snow can be seen in a eulogy written to her by poet Emily H. Woodmansee. In her text, titled "Apostrophe" (1887), Woodmansee makes reference after reference to Snow's poem:

> Free from this most "frail existence"—
> Free to lay "this mortal by"—
> Free to span the starry distance
> To the "royal courts on high,"
> Ransomed spirit! deathless essence!
> Hie thee hence to realms so fair;
> Gain thy Father's radiant presence;
> Greet thy noble Mother there.

While "Invocation" proved to be immensely popular, Snow was also respected for her other works and was called "Zion's

Poetess." However, despite publishing two volumes of poems, Heavenly Mother is not a significant presence in her other works. While a second entry in this anthology shares the trail diary version of a poem where Snow references the early saints praying before "the throne / Of the great eternal mother," this reference was redacted in the published version. The poem "Immortality" makes an indirect reference to Mother, noting how death like a porter will guide the redeemed to the heavenly realm, where they will be free "T' enjoy life's sweet associations, such / As parents, children, husbands, wives and friends— / With Gods and Goddesses—with the noblesse / Of all eternities." The presence of Heavenly Mother here is, at best, an inference.

Beyond the reference made in "Invocation," the clearest language touching Heavenly Mother in Snow's oeuvre comes in "The Ultimatum of Human Life." In this poem, she is visited by the Priesthood, personified as an angel, who seeks to explain the cause of sorrow and the ultimate destiny of humanity. The being explains that the immediate cause of sorrow on Earth is disobedience. Life is an ordeal to prove mankind; but the angel cautions that, nonetheless, "What is done— / All that's attain'd, and what achievements won, / Is for the Parents: All things are their own— / The children now hold nothing but by loan." We are to focus on becoming joint-heirs with Christ through obedience, which will remove sorrow. The Priesthood continues:

> Obedience will the same bright garland weave,
> As it has done for your great Mother, Eve,
> For all her daughters on the earth, who will

All my requirements sacredly fulfill.
And what to Eve, though in her mortal life,
She'd been the first, the tenth, or fiftieth wife?
Whether by fools, consider'd small, or great?
'Twas all the same with her—she prov'd her worth—
She's now the Goddess and the Queen of Earth.

As a result of this education from the Priesthood, the poem's speaker is humbled and recommits herself to live an obedient life, referencing again the will of her Heavenly Parents:

I'll be myself, the humblest saint on earth;
And all that God shall to my care assign,
I'll recognize and use as His, not mine.
Wherever he appoints to me a place,
That will I seek, with diligence, to grace,
And for my Parents, whatso'er my lot,
To work with all my might, and murmur not,
I'll seek their interest, till they send or come,
And as a faithful daughter take me home.

Beyond contributing her poetry to the exploration of such Mormon themes as Heavenly Mother, Snow assisted in the creation of a woman's publication loosely affiliated with the Relief Society, the *Woman's Exponent*. She also wrote a biography of her brother, Lorenzo, and published a collection of letters from her 1872–73 tour of Europe and the Holy Land and five instructional books for children. Notably, she edited and helped prepare a manuscript for Edward W. Tullidge (whose work is also included in *Dove Song*), the *Women of*

Mormondom (1877), which includes extensive discussion of
Heavenly Mother.

"Invocation, or the Eternal Father and Mother." *Poems,
Religious, Historical, and Political*, vol. 1, Latter-day
Saints' Book Depot, 1856, pp. 1–2.

"Immortality." *Poems, Religious, Historical and Political*,
vol. 2, Latter-day Saints' Printing and Publishing
Establishment, 1877, pp. 24–26.

"The Ultimatum of Human Life." *Poems, Religious,
Historical and Political*, vol. 2, Latter-day Saints'
Printing and Publishing Establishment, 1877, pp.
5–10.

Woodmansee, Emily. "Apostrophe." *Latter-day Saints'
Millennial Star*, vol. 50, no. 1, 2 Jan. 1888, p. 16.

JOSEPH L. [LONKING] TOWNSEND was born in
1849 in Canton, Bradford County, Pennsylvania. He grew up
in Ohio (attending high school in Cleveland), Kansas, and
Missouri, and his early education was interspersed with work
on his father's farm. He studied ancient languages at Thayer's
College, then the University of Missouri, and was offered a
professorship in the university's agricultural department;
however, before passing his university examinations, he took ill
with severe fever and chills. He traveled to Salt Lake City in
1872 to improve his health, hoping that a change of climate

would cure him. Within six months, he had joined the LDS church and was later called to live in Payson, Utah, where he met his wife Alta Hancock, with whom he had had 11 children.

Townsend was a business leader in Payson, where he ran a drugstore for 15 years. In 1881, roughly nine years after he arrived in Utah, he interrupted his career to serve a mission to the Southern States. He labored in the Allegheny Mountains region of the States; a place that inspired poetic verse and to which returned in late 1882. Once back in Payson, Townsend continued to develop his business acumen while also working as an educator. He was principal of Payson High School; taught penmanship at both Morgan's Commercial College in Salt Lake City and Brigham Young Academy, where he also taught drawing and manual training; and served as manual training teaching at Salt Lake City High School. Upon retirement, he built a cottage in Payson canyon and made a homestead entry on a tract of woodland in the Uinta National Forest.

As a prolific poet, Townsend wrote lyrics to ten hymns that are in the official 1985 LDS hymnal, including "The Iron Rod," "Choose the Right," "Hope of Israel," and "Oh, What Songs of the Heart."

"What Songs of the Heart." *The Juvenile Instructor*, vol. 14, no. 20, 15 Oct. 1879, p. 240.

EDWARD W. [WHEELOCK] TULLIDGE was Utah's first historian of stature. He wrote a *History of Salt Lake City*

(1886) and many articles on the political and economic history of early Utah in his histories and *Quarterly Magazine* (1880–85). Born in Britain in 1829 into a Wesleyan family, he joined the LDS Church in 1848 and served as a missionary to his own people. In 1854, Tullidge's brief articles in the *Millennial Star* received the attention of Franklin D. Richards and Tullidge was pulled from his work in the mission field to labor in the editorial office under Orson Pratt in 1856.

Convinced that one of his life duties was to write the biography of Joseph Smith, Tullidge traveled to Utah after finishing his mission in 1861. Upon arriving, he received permission from Wilford Woodruff and George A. Smith to use their journals to construct a life of the Prophet, and he was hired to work in the Church Historian's Office. While serving in this capacity, he began to have doubts about the prophetic leadership of Brigham Young and wondered if Young's appointment to the First Presidency was sanctioned by God. In 1864, Tullidge began publishing a literary magazine called the *Peep O'Day*, which contained mostly stories, poems, and essays. However, Tullidge also began suggesting controversial ideas in the magazine—such as the idea that Mormons and Gentiles should develop the West as one people—and the periodical didn't last long.

In 1866, Tullidge left Utah for New York, where he wrote about Mormonism in the magazine, *Galaxy*. When he returned to Utah in 1868, he began publishing articles in a weekly periodical called *The Utah Magazine*. The venture was backed by William Godbe, a Latter-day Saint who soon became dissatisfied with Brigham Young and was convinced that the free and expressive gospel accepted by saints in England was no longer to be found. Godbe and Tullidge quietly committed to work for reform from within the LDS Church. *The Utah Magazine* soon received the Church's attention and those associated with the periodical were called to trial. All but Godbe and Elias L. T. Harrison were forgiven for their acts of dissent, and in front of the high council, Godbe and Harrison opposed the Church leaders and were excommunicated. The magazine was banned from the homes of the Saints and the Godbeite movement floundered without a leader, although it still aimed to rekindle the spirit of the free and inspiring nature of the Church first encountered overseas.

As these events unfolded, Tullidge felt sympathy for his friends and wrote to Brigham Young, admitting his own heterodoxy and severing his ties with the church, but also confessing his love and respect for the Church leader. Following this, Tullidge devoted his time to literary endeavors, writing dramas, essays, histories, and biographies; his first biography was *Life of Brigham Young*; or, *Utah and Her Founders* (1876). He continued the following year with *The Women of Mormondom*, which was edited by Eliza R. Snow.

Women expounded on Mormon belief in a "Father and Mother of creation," They who are the Parents of all mortal spirits. In the book, Tullidge describes Snow's "Invocation" as a choral dramatization of the celestial themes revealed through Joseph Smith. Jesus is the beloved of creation's Father and Mother, Their well tried Son chosen to work out the salvation and exaltation of the human family. For those concerned that giving reverence to Mother would somehow undercut Father, Tullidge notes:

The God-Father is not robbed of his everlasting glory by this maternal completion of himself. It is an expansion both of deity and humanity.

They twain are one God!

The supreme unitarian conception is here; the God-Father and the God-Mother! The grand unity of god is in them—in the divine fatherhood and the divine motherhood—the very beginning and consummation of creation. Not in the God-Father and the God-Son can the unity of the heavens and the earths be worked out; neither with any logic of facts nor of idealities. In them the Masonic trinities; in the everlasting Fathers and the everlasting Mothers the unities of creations.

Tullidge's work also runs deep with Adam-God doctrine, holding the Mother to be Eve, who

plunged down, from the pinnacle of her celestial throne, to earth, to taste of death that her children might have everlasting life. What! should Eve ask Adam to partake of the elements of death first, in such a sacrament! 'Twould have outraged motherhood! Eve partook of that supper of the Lord's death first. She ate of that body and drank of that blood.

Tullidge's final work was the project he felt called to begin as a missionary, *Life of Joseph the Prophet*; soon after finishing it, he joined the RLDS church and began writing *Tullidge's Quarterly Magazine, of Utah, Her Founders, Her Enterprises, and Her Civilization*. He wrote additional histories until his death in 1894.

"Marriage." *The Latter-day Saints' Millennial Star*, vol. 19, no. 41, 1857, p. 656.

The Women of Mormondom. Tullidge & Crandall, 1877, p. 187–200.

J. H. [JOSEPH HARVEY] WARD was born in London, Ontario, Canada in 1843. His father was a millwright who travelled throughout eastern Canada for work and ended up in Michigan. After his father passed away and his mother remarried, Ward was taken in by his father's extended family in Minnesota. As a bookworm, he did odd jobs to acquire more books and contributed articles, prose, and poetry to the *Shakopee Argus*, much to the behest of his uncle, the periodical's editor.

As an adult, Ward visited fur traders and became a volunteer soldier in the Civil War, where he was wounded, became a hospital steward, and was recommended by chaplains to study for the Christian ministry. With that in mind, Ward became a Sabbath school teacher and superintendent of the Maxwell Street Mission in Chicago. He married and had a child, but his wife died shortly thereafter.

In 1872, Ward converted to Mormonism and traveled to Utah. He became an LDS apologist, writing a series of works in the 1880s to address the doubts of the rising generation of Latter-day Saints. Along this vein, his 1883 work, *The Hand of Providence*, details God's purported involvement in history from the time of the "great apostasy to the restoration of the gospel" at the hands of Joseph Smith. And his 1884 book, *Absurdities of*

Infidelity, and the Harmony of the Gospel with Science and History,
intends to take "the leading arguments of infidel writers, and to
refute them by well-known facts," many of which were
geological and astronomical in nature.

In *Ballads of Life* (1886), Ward collected poems he had
written in a variety of circumstances over the past 26 years,
including those composed "in the old-fashioned farm-house, in
the bustling railroad depot, on the broad and lonely prairie, in
far northern wilds, amid the children of the forest, and some
even in a soldier's tent, with a drum-head for a writing desk,
while watching at the bedside of a wounded comrade." He also
translated from famous European poets. Some of his poems
were set to music (e.g., "The Great Question" and "Utah, the
Queen of the West").

"To Unseen Friends." *Ballads of Life.* Joseph Hyrum
Parry & Co., 1886, pp. 197–98.

ORSON F. [FERGUSON] WHITNEY, born in Salt
Lake City in 1855, was an oddity in the Mormon community.
In an era when male church leadership and membership
consisted largely of self-made craftsmen and pioneers, Whitney
was not a frontiersman. Besides a short stint as a railroad
worker when he was 13, he didn't labor with his hands. He was
also among a new generation of Latter-day Saints who didn't
know the Prophet or the eastern states from which the Saints
came: he was, rather, a child of Deseret who longed to be an
actor, a musician, and later on a writer, poet, and scholar.

As a youth, Whitney cared little for spirituality and religion. He was baptized at 11 and held no priesthood office until he was ordained an elder at age 18. At 21, he was called to serve a mission, a responsibility he accepted despite his lack of preparation and the way the call intervened with his theatrical aspirations. He admitted that, at the beginning of his service, he was a lackluster missionary, more interested in newspaper correspondence than the work of ministry. An intense religious experience catalyzed a change in his attitude: he witnessed the Savior's suffering in Gethsemane and spoke with the resurrected Christ in a dream. Whitney blossomed into a successful missionary when sent to work alone in Ohio, where his talents as a writer and orator were markedly enhanced.

Upon returning from his mission, Whitney secured a position at the *Deseret News*. Many of his acquaintances doubted that he would remain committed to gospel principles, but he proved them wrong. To his great surprise during a church meeting, he was called and sustained as bishop of the Salt Lake 18th ward. The surprise wasn't just because he was young and no one had informed him of the calling; rather, it caught him off guard because he wasn't married and bishops were supposed to have a spouse. While he resolved that problem the following year (in 1879), when he married Zina Beal Smoot, he didn't serve for long before he accepted the call to work for the editorial department of the *Millennial Star* in London. While away from his wife, his second child was born and died. He returned to his familial and pastoral duties in 1884 and left the *Deseret News* to work as a treasurer in the local government. His career oscillated thereafter between political and academic positions, and he sought to find time for his families (Whitney practiced polygamy, marrying May Wells) and his congregation; he also pursued his desire to publish, writing some successful biographical, historical, and literary works, of which his epic, *Elias*, is perhaps the most recognized today.

Whitney was caught up in the issues that affected his community. During the heat of the anti-polygamy crusade, he was the Mormon appointed to hold LDS services at the penitentiary, visiting and preaching to the apostles and members of the First Presidency. Few know this, but Whitney was actually the person selected to read Wilford Woodruff's polygamy-ending manifesto aloud to the saints assembled at the October 1890 General Conference. After the official practice ended, Whitney sought protections for aged polygamists. He played a leading role in the great woman suffrage debate, during which his speeches were published in pamphlets; and he successfully worked to secure women's right to vote, arguing against opponents such as prominent LDS intellectual B. H. Roberts. Women had always voted in the church, Whitney observed, so why shouldn't they be able to vote in their nation?

At the turn of the century, Whitney served in the Church Historian's office before being called as an apostle by President Joseph F. Smith. The Quorum of the Twelve had three vacancies, due to the death of one apostle and two others resigning over a dispute regarding the 1890 Manifesto. Whitney's oratory and writing skills were put to good use in this calling, as he preached across the stakes of Zion, published pastoral articles in church periodicals, and delivered spiritual lectures, which were broadcast over the KSL radio station.

While Whitney's literary works touch a little upon the concept of Heavenly Mother (She's only addressed in *Elias* and his early poem "What is Life?"), no LDS general authority has spoken as prolifically about Her; She appears in nearly 40 of his published sermons, lectures, General Conference addresses, and other writings. He even entered a public debate in the newspapers when a protestant pastor refused to let "O My Father" be sung at a funeral.

> "What is Life?" *The Latter-day Saints' Millenial Star*, vol. 44, no. 45, 1882, p. 713–14. Reprinted in *The Poetical Writings of Orson F. Whitney: Poems and Poetic Prose*. 1889, pp. 113–15.

> *Elias: An Epic of the Ages*. Author's Jubilee Edition, Knickerbocker Press, 1904, pp. 11, 42, 100, 103–04.

JABEZ WOODARD was born in 1821 to James Woodard, the gardener of Sir Hew Dalrymple, Baronet at Hebrew, in the Parish of Aldenham in the county of Hertfordshire, England. Woodard grew up and became gardener himself. He married a ladies' maid on the same estate, Ann Granger, and had two daughters, Eleanor and Harriet. They joined the LDS church in late 1849, and soon after Woodard was called to assist Lorenzo Snow in opening up the Italian mission. Fluent in German, Spanish, and Italian, Woodard was a logical choice.

He returned to his family in 1854 and prepared to take them to Utah. On the way there, his daughter Harriet contracted cholera and died at the Kansas Camping Grounds. They reached Utah in the Fall of 1854, settled in West Jordan, and soon had a son they named David. In 1857, Brigham Young called Woodard to assist Lorenzo Snow again, this time with the Swiss-German mission. Woodard accepted the call, leaving his family in difficult conditions, with Ann working as a seamstress and Eleanor milking cows to help make ends meet. During his time away, Woodard presided over the mission.

When he returned home in 1861, his family was called to help with the "Muddy Mission," a territory southwest of St. George, near today's Logandale and Overton, Nevada. Woodard taught school there, receiving produce as pay, and Ann gleaned cotton and wool and knitted. The area struggled agriculturally, famine hit, and Woodard's family nearly starved to death. In 1869, Woodard returned to Utah to find work; he took a job feeding cattle in Morgan County. One day while working, he grew ill and died suddenly on March 2, 1870. Ann didn't receive word of his death until he was already buried in Milton, Utah.

"Our Existence—Past, Present, and Future." *The Mormon*, vol. 3, no. 24, 1857, p. 1.

CONTRIBUTOR NOTES

This section offers details about the lives of the contemporary Mormon poets and visual artists whose work we've featured in the anthology. It also lists publication information for previously published work.

EMILY HARRIS ADAMS is a connoisseur of playgrounds, crayon brands, and varieties of apples. She is an author, a military wife, and the proud mother of IVF twins and three (currently) frozen embryos. Her book, *For Those with Empty Arms*, is available from Amazon, Deseret Book, and Barnes and Noble.

DAVID ALLRED, to his surprise, met the Goddess reading about her work in the world. He reflects that he has reverenced Lady Wisdom his whole life. He is a professor in the natural sciences. Knowing her sustains him in dry times. He is not surprised to find her image in the good strong women around him. He is married to Janice Allred.

"Invocation." *Sunstone*, no. 166, 2012.

JANICE ALLRED is an independent scholar who speaks and writes on theological topics. The author of *God the Mother and Other Theological Essays*, she has a chapter in *Voices for Equality: Ordain Women and Resurgent Mormon Feminism* and has published in *Dialogue, A Journal of Mormon Thought*, *Sunstone*, and *Mormon Women's Forum: An LDS Feminist Quarterly*.

KRISTINE ROSE BARRETT is an author and occupational therapist who lives in Colorado. Her poem was the direct result of her dear friendships with Sonia Johnson, who was the president of Mormons for the ERA, and Linda Sillitoe, the greatly gifted and insight-abounding poet and writer, whose work also appears in this volume.

> "To Mother in Heaven." *Exponent II*, vol. 7, no. 2, 1981. Reprinted in *Exponent II*, vol. 30, no. 4, 2011, p. 34.

M. SHAYNE BELL received a Creative Writing Fellowship from the National Endowment for the Arts (1991). His poem, "One Hundred Years of Russian Revolution," was a finalist for the Rhysling Award (1989). His poetry has been published in *Modern Haiku, Tinywords, The Fibonacci Review, The Ghazal Page, Shot Glass Journal, Dialogue, Sunstone, Amazing Stories, Asimov's*, etc. Bell also publishes science fiction, and has been a finalist for the Hugo and Nebula awards. He received a first place Writers of the Future award (1990).

> "I Looked for Her." *The Ghazal Page*, 15 February 2016.

JOANNA BROOKS is an award-winning scholar and
author or editor of nine books including *Mormon Feminism:
Essential Writings* (Oxford, 2016) and *Decolonizing Mormonism*,
with Gina Colvin (University of Utah, 2018).

> "Invocation / Benediction." *Exponent II*, vol. 30, no. 3,
> 2010, p. 19. Reprinted in *Mormon Feminism:
> Essential Writings*. Oxford University Press, 2016.

> "She Who Has No Name." *Exponent II*, vol. 37, no. 1,
> 2017.

MARKAY BROWN, St George, Utah, was born an addict
to the written word. She won first place for her manuscript,
Eve's Child, in the 2014 Utah Original Writing Competition,
Book-length Collection of Poetry, judged by Richard Howard
of Columbia University. Her poems have appeared in *Segullah*,
Provo/Orem Word, *15 Bytes*, *Encore*, *Southern Quill*, and
elsewhere. She serves as president of Redrock Writers, a
chapter of the Utah State Poetry Society.

> "Mothers in Heaven." *A Mother Here: Art and Poetry
> Contest* (amotherhere.com), 2014.

CHERYL BRUNO has a Bachelor's degree in Recreation
Management from Greensboro College. She served an 18-
month LDS mission in Quebec, Canada, then entered the
"Mommy track." For 15 years most of her energy went into
raising her eight children, with occasional part-time work as a

swim coach. In 2012 Cheryl started working as an Aquatics Director in Seattle, WA. She now leads a YMCA after-school program in Ogden, Utah.

MARILYN BUSHMAN-CARLTON's newest book, *Worthy*, a biography, is a National Indie Excellence Awards finalist. Her three poetry books have won awards from the Association of Mormon Letters, the *Comstock Review*, and the Utah Arts Council. She has contributed to numerous journals and anthologies including *Fire in the Pasture*, *Discoveries: Two Centuries of Poems by Mormon Women*, and *Baring Witness: 36 Mormon Women Talk Candidly about Love, Sex, and Marriage*. *Pulchritudinous and Other Ways to Say Beautiful*, a book of children's poetry, is dedicated to her sixteen grandchildren.

ALEX CALDIERO is a sonosopher, polyartist, and scholar of humanities and intermedia. Publications include *Sound Weave* (Differential Records), *sonosuono* (Elik), *Poetry Is Wanted Here!* (Dream Garden Press), *Some Love* (Signature Books), and *Who is the Dancer, What is the Dance* (saltfront). He's co-founder of Arba Sicula, society for Sicilian language & culture; and has been featured in *Dictionary of the Avant-gardes* (Macmillan, London), the poetry anthology *Fire in the Pasture* (Peculiar Pages), and a documentary *Alex Caldiero ... in Life, in Sound*. He's Senior Artist in Residence at Utah Valley University.

"*U latti dâ matri* [The Milk of the Mother]." CSSSS, Catania, Sicily, 1980.

TYLER CHADWICK, an award-winning poet, essayist, editor, and teacher, received his BS in English from Weber State University, his MA in English from National University, and his PhD in English and the Teaching of English from Idaho State. Besides *Dove Song*, he has two books to his name: another anthology, *Fire in the Pasture: 21st Century Mormon Poets* (Peculiar Pages, 2011), and a collection of poetry and essays, *Field Notes on Language and Kinship* (Mormon Artists Group, 2013). He lives in Ogden, Utah, with his wife, Jess, and their four daughters.

"[Goddess looking up, sowing mercy]." *BYU Studies Quarterly*, vol. 56, no. 1, 2017, p. 74.

MARDEN CLARK should have been locked up long ago, but since, by some bureaucratic oversight, he was allowed to mate and reproduce, the cat is out of the bag and the toothpaste is out of the tube and the cat is playing with the toothpaste so ... be careful what you put on your toothbrush tonight. By way of prophylaxis, Mr. Clark is publishing these poems under a pseudonym; if you meet him in the street, pretend you do not see him and he will gratefully pass you by in anonymity. Whatever you do, don't encourage him. Two is enough.

HARLOW CLARK's first published poem after high school (10 years after) was a devotional piece about Gethsemane in the Seattle Arts Council's non-devotional annual, *Image*. He was first poetry editor of *Irreantum*, and his work has appeared in

Irreantum, *Dialogue*, and *Sunstone*, in local newspapers, and on *Wilderness Interface Zone*, *A Motley Vision*, and *Dawning of a Brighter Day*, which all sounds more impressive than it is.

CAITLIN CONNOLLY is an artist, a wife to a guitarist, a musician, and a creative enthusiast. Born and raised in Utah, the only girl in a family with three brothers, she grew up coloring the walls with crayons while becoming well acquainted with boy scouts and power tools. She graduated from the University of Utah in 2009 with a BFA, emphasizing in Painting and Drawing, and has been passionately pursuing and cultivating her creative path since that time. She currently lives in Provo, Utah, with her husband and two dogs, and is a new mother to two baby boys. She loves spending time with her family, in her studio, touring on the road with her husband, reading, writing, and watching a good TV show.

MELISSA DALTON-BRADFORD is an award-winning author of books (*Global Mom: A Memoir; On Loss and Living Onward*), essays (*Transitions*), and poetry (*Fire in the Pasture*). She holds a BA in German and an MA in Comparative Literature, both from Brigham Young University. She and her husband, Randall, have lived in Hong Kong and Vienna, and have raised their four children in Oslo, Paris, Munich, Singapore, Geneva, and Frankfurt.

"Phoning Home." *A Mother Here: Art and Poetry Contest* (amotherhere.com), 2014.

GALEN DARA likes monsters, mystics, dead things, and extremely ripe apricots. She won the 2016 World Fantasy Award and has been nominated for the Hugo, the Chesley, The Locus, and other various and sundry accolades. When she's not making art you can find her at the edge of the Sonoran Desert climbing mountains and hanging out with a friendly conglomerate of humans and animals. You can follow her on facebook, instagram, and twitter @galendara. galendara.com

DEJA EARLEY lives in Auburn, Alabama, with her husband, her daughter, and a lot of books. Her own book, a collection of poetry titled *To the Mormon Newlyweds Who Thought the Bellybutton Was Somehow Involved*, will be released in 2018 from Signature Books.

"Of Thy Womb." *A Mother Here: Art and Poetry Contest* (amotherhere.com), 2014.

SIMON PETER EGGERTSEN was born in Kansas, raised in Utah, schooled in Virginia and England. His verses have been published in *Nimrod*, *Vallum*, *New Millennium Writings*, *Spoon River Poetry Review*, *Ekphrasis*, *Weber: The Contemporary West*, *Dialogue*, and elsewhere. A set of his poems won the Irreantum Poetry Prize (2012); others have been shortlisted for the ARC Poem of the Year (Canada, 2013) and the Fish Poetry Prize (Ireland, 2013, 2014) and declared finalists for the Far Horizon Poetry Prize (Malahat (Canada), 2014), Open Season Poetry Prize (Malahat, 2017), and the Pablo Neruda Poetry Prize (Nimrod, 2009).

DENISE GASSER is a mixed media artist, born and raised near the mountains of Utah. She lived in the San Francisco Bay Area for a time, before moving to her current home in Vancouver, BC. This journey north has added depth and maturity to her work as she has immersed herself in the natural wonders of the Northwest Coast. Denise shares her home studio with her architect husband and their three young, and very busy, sons.

MAXINE HANKS is a theologian and historian who writes and lectures on gender studies in religion. She has published several books and articles on Mormon history and studies, including *Women and Authority: Re-emerging Mormon Feminism*. She studied English and rhetoric with Arthur Henry King at BYU, majored and lectured in Gender Studies at the U of U, and did graduate studies in religion at Harvard and elsewhere. She has published poetry in *Ellipsis*, *Sunstone*, *MWF Quarterly*, and *Stone Startled*.

> "Medusa's Prayer." *Mormon Women's Forum Quarterly*,
> vol. 3, no. 2, 1992, p. 57.

LISA BOLIN HAWKINS is a writer and editor, and formerly taught writing and law at BYU. She wrote the poems included in this anthology after the chaos of the Utah International Women's Year meetings in 1977. She has published poetry in the *Ensign*, *Exponent II*, *Sunstone*, and *BYU Studies*, and blogs at sisterlykindness.com.

"Another Prayer." *Exponent II* vol. 6, 1980, p. 16.
Reprinted in *Exponent II* (ten-year retrospective),
vol. 10, no. 1, 1984, p. 11, and *Mormon Feminism:
Essential Writings*. Oxford University Press, 2016.

"Let My Sisters Do for Me." *Dialogue: A Journal of
Mormon Thought*, vol. 13, no. 4, 1980, p. 57.
Reprinted in *Mormon Feminism: Essential Writings*.
Oxford University Press, 2016.

ASHLEY MAE HOILAND is the author of *One Hundred
Birds Taught Me to Fly*. She has published several children's
books and is the illustrator of *Mother's Milk* by Rachel Hunt
Steenblik. She founded the We Brave Women movement,
which is an initiative to tell the stories of brave women around
the world. She currently lives in Palo Alto with her husband
and three small children.

"[In the temple]." *One Hundred Birds Taught Me to Fly:
The Art of Seeking God*. Neal A. Maxwell Institute
for Religious Scholarship, 2016, p. 5.

"Some Women Whose Stories I Have Known or Am
Getting to Know." *One Hundred Birds Taught Me to
Fly: The Art of Seeking God*. Neal A. Maxwell
Institute for Religious Scholarship, 2016, p. 166.

TRISH HOPKINSON is author of three chapbooks and
has been published in several anthologies and journals,
including *Stirring*, *Pretty Owl Poetry*, and *The Penn Review*. You
can follow Hopkinson on her blog where she shares

information on how to write, publish, and participate in the greater poetry community at trishhopkinson.com.

> "Three atheists and a Mormon walk into a café." *Crab Fat Magazine*, July 2017.

SUSAN ELIZABETH HOWE is a retired BYU professor of English. Her poetry collection *Salt* is available from Signature Books. Her poems have recently appeared in *Poetry*, *Western Humanities Review*, and *Atlanta Review*. She lives with her husband Cless Young in Ephraim, Utah.

EMMA JAY won second place in the A Mother Here: Art and Poetry Contest for her poem "O."

> "O." *A Mother Here: Art and Poetry Contest* (amotherhere.com), 2014.

MELODY NEWEY JOHNSON's award-winning poems have appeared in *Irreantum*, *Segullah*, *Exponent II*, *Utah Voices 2012*, *Utah Sings*, and elsewhere. She is a featured literary artist at Artists of Utah's *15 Bytes*. In addition to writing she enjoys gardening with her spouse and building sheet forts with grandchildren.

> "Missing God." *A Mother Here: Art and Poetry Contest* (amotherhere.com), 2014.

> "The River You Always Knew" and "Word of God." *A Mother Here: Art and Poetry Contest* (amotherhere.com), 2014.

"Mother Work." *Exponent II*, vol. 38, no. 1, 2018.

"How Long the Call." *Psaltery & Lyre*, 8 January 2018.

"Mother's Milk." *Rational Faiths*, 9 September 2013.

"Heavenly Mother Sings." *Rational Faiths*, 28 February 2013.

TINA LINDSAY grew up on the east coast, but quickly became a Utah native after attending BYU for seven years and receiving her law degree. She practiced bankruptcy law for several years until she had her daughter and decided to pursue her passion for writing. In 2013, she made the difficult decision to leave the Mormon church. One of her central issues with the church was the scarcity of any real female role models for her daughter to look up to. She wanted her to understand that there was divine feminine that was just as important as any masculine god. She hopes that her poem helps achieve that.

"My Mother Is ..." *A Mother Here: Art and Poetry Contest* (amotherhere.com), 2014.

TIMOTHY LIU's *Luminous Debris: New & Selected Legerdemain* (1992–2017) will be published in 2018. A reader of occult esoterica, he lives in Manhattan and Woodstock, New York. timothyliu.net

CONNER McKINNON attended Brigham Young University and majored in English. His poetry and prose have been published and performed across various anthologies and venues, most notably when featured as a special guest on Oprah for his essay on preserving the stories of Holocaust victims. He lives in Salt Lake City, Utah, where the mountains offer no shortage of poetic inspiration.

"To Her." *A Mother Here: Art and Poetry Contest* (amotherhere.com), 2014.

DESIREE MILLER is a non-binary person who spends their free time learning more about brain development so they can be a better parent and human. After the policy changes, they stepped away from the church and now commune with God by marching and protesting in the streets.

"Yin." *A Mother Here: Art and Poetry Contest* (amotherhere.com), 2014.

TIFFANY MOSS was born, raised, and currently resides along the Wasatch Front. She feels intimately connected with the land and is happiest when outside. Her interests include reading, writing, hiking, kayaking, and eating good food with friends and family. She earned a BA in humanities with an English emphasis from Brigham Young University. She has previously written about women's issues for *Sunstone* and *Exponent II*.

"Flesh and Bone." *A Mother Here: Art and Poetry Contest* (amotherhere.com), 2014.

LYNDE MADSEN MOTT received a BFA in illustration from BYU in 1997. She has been a Jane-of-all-Trades since, working as a historical illustrator, muralist, public speaker, costume designer, health coach, and emotional release facilitator. She lives in Pleasant Grove, Utah, with her band teacher husband and thespian-focused teenage son while her twins, Jonathon and Daniel, are serving missions in Honduras and Peru. Every room in her home, including the garage and her husband's 1969 VW bus, has a colorful mural. No surface is safe with Lynde. YouTube: "Lynde Mott's Home Tour."

MARGARET RAMPTON MUNK graduated from the University of Utah, and then did graduate work in government at Harvard. She met Russell Munk while working in Washington, D.C., following her freshman year of college, and they later married while in graduate school. Russ' work took them to Japan and then to the Philippines. Meg taught political science classes at Jesuit universities in both Tokyo and Manila. While in the Philippines, the Munks adopted Laura and Dan, and Meg's focus became her family. After returning to the United States, the Munks adopted Andrew. Most of Meg's poems, including several published in *Exponent II*, dealt with her personal experiences. In 1983, Meg was diagnosed with ovarian cancer. After surgery and a year of chemotherapy she wrote the poem sequence "One Year." Her collection of poetry, *So Far*, was published just before her death in 1986.

"First Grief." *Exponent II*, vol. 5, no. 1, 1978, p. 17. Reprinted in *Mormon Feminism: Essential Writings*. Oxford University Press, 2016.

DANNY NELSON's interest in Heavenly Mother began at a Stake Conference in which a High Councilor expressed his belief that Heavenly Mother was responsible for the colors in the rainbow. Published in *The Fob Bible*, *Monsters & Mormons*, and others, Danny has long been an advocate for Mormon literary art. Danny currently lives in Salt Lake City with his husband and two small dogs.

"Creation." *The Fob Bible*. Peculiar Pages, 2011, p. 3.

CALVIN OLSEN holds an MFA in Creative Writing from Boston University, where he received a Robert Pinsky Global Fellowship. His poetry and translations have appeared in *International Poetry Review*, *The Missouri Review Online*, *The London Magazine*, *Tupelo Quarterly*, *Columbia*, and others. He lives in Chapel Hill, North Carolina, where he is poetry editor for *The Carolina Quarterly*.

"Rejoinder" and "Veil." *A Mother Here: Art and Poetry Contest* (amotherhere.com), 2014.

REBEKAH ORTON attended Brigham Young University and earned an MA in creative writing. Since then, she has taught college English and published short fiction, poems, and essays in periodicals including *Switchback*, *J Journal*, and *Brain, Child Magazine*. She currently lives in Vienna, Austria, with her husband and three children.

"Heavenly Mother Eats Carbs" and "It's Possible I'm Projecting." *A Mother Here: Art and Poetry Contest* (amotherhere.com), 2014.

BLAIRE OSTLER is a leading voice at the intersection of Mormonism, feminism, and transhumanism. She is a Board Member and former CEO of the Mormon Transhumanist Association, the world's largest advocacy network for the ethical use of technology and religion to expand human abilities. She is currently pursuing a second degree in philosophy with an emphasis in gender studies. Blaire and husband Drew reside in Utah with their three children.

CAROL CLARK OTTESEN graduated from Springville High School in 1948 and went on to receive a bachelor's degree in music and German from Brigham Young University. Carol married her high school sweetheart, Sterling E. Ottesen, September 5, 1952 in the Salt Lake Temple. Carol and Sterling moved to Southern California early in their marriage where Sterling completed dental school. Carol and her husband lived near the beach for 42 years, raising six children and sweeping sand from the corners of the kitchen. Carol received a master's degree in English from Cal State University Dominguez Hills, and later became a faculty member of the same university. In 1995 Carol and Sterling moved to Mapleton, Utah, where she taught English and Native American Studies at Brigham Young University.

"The Father and the Mother." *Sunstone*, no. 85, 1991, p. 51.

S.E. PAGE has an MS and certification in Secondary English and keeps her quill sharp by scribbling stories and poems and by editing *Young Ravens Literary Review*. She blogs about her creative projects at iffymagic.com.

JIM PAPWORTH retired from teaching at BYU–Idaho in 2016. Currently he helps Anne raise their two youngest sons, cooks, cleans, and works with great pleasure restoring a 1968 VW Transporter, you know, for fun.

> "The Seven Songs of Creation" and "The Woman Whose Husband Finds Heart-Shaped Stones." *A Mother Here: Art and Poetry Contest* (amotherhere.com), 2014.

LINDSAY HANSEN PARK is a women's rights activist, a feminist blogger, and an advocate against gender violence. She co-founded Utah For Congo to raise awareness for rape survivors and is currently heavily involved in the Mormon Feminist movement. Lindsay is the Assistant Director for the Sunstone Education Foundation and the founder of the Feminist Mormon Housewives Podcast. She blogs for *FeministMormon-Housewives.org* about women's issues. Her work has been referenced by the *New York Times*, the *Wall Street Journal*, *NPR*, *Quartz Magazine*, and many other Utah publications. She and her family live in Stansbury Park, Utah, where she raises three beautiful kiddos, gardens, and rages against the machine.

"Where is Mother?" *Exponent II*, vol. 31, no. 3, 2011, p. 12.

DAYNA PATTERSON earned an MA in Literature from Texas State University and an MFA in Creative Writing from Western Washington University, where she served as managing editor of *Bellingham Review*. She is the founding editor-in-chief of *Psaltery & Lyre* and poetry editor for *Exponent II*. daynapatterson.com

> "Proselytizing by a Marian Shrine in Québec." *Loose Threads*. Flutter Press, 2010. Reprinted in *Exponent II*, vol. 31, no. 2, 2011, p. 39.

> "Eloher," "Harvest Dance," "Mother Has a Degree in Exterior Design," and "Whale Watching." *A Mother Here: Art and Poetry Contest* (amotherhere.com), 2014.

> "New Moon." *Psaltery & Lyre*, 8 May 2014.

> "If Mother Braids a Waterfall." *Segullah*, 14 August 2017.

CAROL LYNN PEARSON is the author of over 40 books and plays. Her Mormon audience knows her ongoing work on LGBT issues as well as her work for women, a major theme being our need to acknowledge God as both Mother and Father. She wrote and performed over 300 times internationally a one-woman play, "Mother Wove the Morning." Carol Lynn is an active member of her ward in California.

"Family of Light." *Daughters of Light*. Bookcraft, 1973.

"Blessing," "Parent Friends," and "Within." *A Widening View*. Bookcraft, 1983.

"A Motherless House." *Women and Authority*, edited by Maxine Hanks. Signature Books, 1992, pp. 232–33. Reprinted in *Mormon Feminism: Essential Writings*. Oxford University Press, 2016.

"Support Group" and "In Celebration of the First Menstruation." *Women I Have Known and Been*. Gold Leaf Press, 1992.

STEVEN L. PECK is a BYU Biologist, but moonlights as an award-winning novelist, poet, and short story writer. His poetry has appeared in *Abyss & Apex*, *BYU Studies*, *Dialogue*, *Irreantum*, *Pedestal Magazine*, *Prairie Schooner*, *Red Rock Review*, and other places. His poetry collection, *Incorrect Astronomy*, was published by Aldrich Press in 2013.

"My Turn on Earth." *By Common Consent*, 30 May 2012. Reprinted in *Gilda Trillim: Shepherdess of Rats*. Roundfire Books, 2017.

JONATHON PENNY is a professor of literature at RIT Dubai, where he also chairs the Sciences and Liberal Arts department. He is Vice-President of Mormon Scholars in the Humanities, a sometime rock vocalist, an amateur theologian, and a speculative historian. He and his wife, Wendy Cahoon, have three sons—two of whom are now grown men—and a daughter-in-law. These last two facts are both pleasant and discombobulating, but like the best incremental refrains.

"Song to be sung in times of famine, fear, and desolation." *Psaltery & Lyre*, 9 June 2014.

MARILÈNE PHIPPS held fellowships at the Guggenheim Foundation, and at Harvard's Bunting Institute, W.E.B. Du Bois Institute, and the Center for the Study of World Religions. She won the 1993 Grolier Poetry Prize. Her collection, *Crossroads and Unholy Water*, won the Crab Orchard Poetry Prize. Her collection, *The Company of Heaven*, won the Iowa Short Fiction Award. Her work is published in England by Carcanet Press, and in American anthologies such as *The Beacon Best*, *Ploughshares*, *River Styx*. She was the editor of the *Jack Kerouac: Collected Poems* for The Library of America. Her memoir/conversion-story, *Mahogany*, is to be published by Calumet Editions in early 2018.

ELIZABETH PINBOROUGH is a writer who lives in Salt Lake City. She co-edits the online arts and literary journal *Young Ravens Literary Review*. Her work has appeared online in *Wilderness Interface Zone* and *Psaltery & Lyre*, and in print in *Dialogue: A Journal of Mormon Thought*, *Exponent II*, and *Fire in the Pasture: 21st Century Mormon Poets*. She edited the book *Habits of Being: Mormon Women's Material Culture*, published by *Exponent II*.

THALIA POPE recently graduated from Brigham Young University with a degree in English and minors in Visual Design and Digital Humanities & Technology. Her interests include print layout design, queer and gender studies, and volunteering at her local children's advocacy center. While Thalia currently freelances as a graphic designer, she plans to find work in sexual assault victim advocacy and will be certified as an international ESL instructor in July.

"Unspoken Prayer." *Segullah*, August 2017.

ELISA EASTWOOD PULIDO teaches World Religions at Brigham Young University Salt Lake Center. She holds a PhD in Religious Studies from Claremont Graduate University and an MFA in Writing from the School of the Art Institute of Chicago. Her poems have appeared in *Fire in the Pasture: 21st Century Mormon Poets* and in many journals in the U.S. and in the U.K., including *The North American Review*, *River Styx*, *Rhino*, *The New Welsh Review*, *Interchange*, *Tor House Newsletter*, and many others.

"Sightings: The Heavenly Mother in North Central Texas." *A Mother Here: Art and Poetry Contest* (amotherhere.com), 2014.

MARTIN PULIDO received a BA in English and philosophy from BYU, and co-authored the *BYU Studies* article, "A Mother There: A Survey of Historical Teachings about Mother in Heaven," with David Paulsen. He has presented at academic conferences on the historical development and doctrinal impetuses of the belief in the early Mormon church, as well as social applications of the doctrine. Believing conversations regarding Heavenly Mother in the LDS church could be furthered greater through art, he organized the *A Mother Here: Art and Poetry Contest* with co-chair Caroline Kline in 2014, and has conducted research into early Mormon poetry referring to Heavenly Mother. He and his brother Joseph earned a 2015 Watty award for their science fiction novel, *Herald of Fury*.

"Windows." *A Mother Here: Art and Poetry Contest* (amotherhere.com), 2014.

ROBERT A. REES is Director of Mormon Studies and Visiting Professor at Graduate Theological Union in Berkeley. Previously he taught at UCLA, UC Santa Cruz, and UC Berkeley and was a Fulbright Professor of American Studies in the Baltics. His poetry, which has appeared in various journals, magazines, and anthologies, has been gathered in *Waiting for Morning* (Zarahemla Press, 2017). He recently completed *American Dreams*, a play about the American Renaissance and is working on a play about Ezra Pound.

"Mother." *Exponent II*, vol. 33, no. 1, 2013, p. 7.

"Her." *A Mother Here: Art and Poetry Contest* (amotherhere.com), 2014.

WILL REGER has been writing poetry since the 7th grade, published both in print and online, most recently with *Front Porch Review*, *Chiron Review*, *VerseWrights.com*, *The Literary Nest*, and *Paterson Literary Review*. He is a founding member of the CU (Champaign–Urbana) Poetry Group (cupoetry.com). More of his poetry can be found at twitter.com/wmreger.

J. KIRK RICHARDS attributes much of his love for the arts to an early emphasis on musical training in his parents' home. Turning then from music to visual arts, Kirk studied with painters Clayton Williams, Bruce Hixson Smith, Patrick Devonas, Hagen Haltern, Gary and Jennifer Barton, James Christensen, Wulf Barsch, Joe Ostraff, and others. Two years in Rome influenced Richards' palette, which often consists of subdued browns and rusts. He is best known for his contributions to the BYU Museum of Art exhibit *Beholding Salvation: The Life of Christ in Word and Image*; for his contributions to Helen Whitney's PBS Frontline Documentary, *The Mormons: An American Experience*; for the cover image of Jeffrey R. Holland's book, *Broken Things to Mend*; and for his imagery on the cover of *BYU Studies Quarterly* and in the *Ensign*, *Liahona*, and Upper Room publications. Kirk and his wife, Amy Tolk Richards, have four creative children. They split their time between their home in Woodland Hills, Utah, and their country studio in the small town of Redmond, Utah.

JIM RICHARDS's poems have been nominated for Best New Poets, two Pushcart Prizes, and have appeared recently in

Poetry Northwest, *Prairie Schooner*, *Southern Poetry Review*, *South Carolina Review*, and *Juked*. He teaches literature and creative writing at BYU–Idaho and is a recipient of a fellowship from the Idaho Commission on the Arts. jim-richards.com

> "Octave." *A Mother Here: Art and Poetry Contest* (amotherhere.com), 2014.

TAYLOR ROUANZION has a BA in English from Brigham Young University with a minor in editing. She served as Editor-in-Chief for *Inscape* (BYU's Creative Writing Journal) and an Editorial Assistant at the BYU Humanities Publication Center. After college, she was a Technical Writer/Editor at an engineering company. Now she is focused on her writing and raising her five-year-old son. In addition to poetry, she also writes young adult novels. She was born and raised in Oklahoma and currently lives in Lexington, Kentucky.

> "A Mother's Comfort." *A Mother Here: Art and Poetry Contest* (amotherhere.com), 2014.

LORETTA RANDALL SHARP earned BA and MA degrees from BYU, and established the creative writing program at Interlochen Arts Academy in Michigan. She has received Fulbright fellowships to India (1984) and Pakistan (1988), and a Klingenstein fellowship, Columbia University (1987–88).

> "Divestiture." *Exponent II*, vol. 13, no. 2, 1987, p. 9.

BONNIE SHIFFLER-OLSEN is a poly-artist, humanitarian, and co-founder of Rock Canyon Poets. Her work has appeared in *Quarterly West*, *Dialogue: A Journal of Mormon Thought*, *Rust+Moth*, *Crab Fat*, *Peculiar: A Queer Literary Journal*, *Nuclear Impact: Broken Atoms in Our Hands*, and elsewhere. She is the mother of four children, and resides in Provo, Utah.

> "Three atheists and a Mormon walk into a café." *Crab Fat Magazine*, July 2017.

LINDA SILLITOE graduated from the University of Utah and worked as a journalist for the *Deseret News*, *Utah Holiday* magazine, and *The New York Times*. Her books include two poetry collections, *Crazy for Living* (Signature Books, 1993) and *Owning the Moon* (Signature Books, 2018).

> "Song of Creation." *Dialogue: A Journal of Mormon Thought*, vol. 12, no. 4, 1979, p. 95. Reprinted in *Harvest: Contemporary Mormon Poems*, Signature Books, 1989, and *Crazy for Living*, Signature Books, 1993.

REBECCA SORGE loves telling stories and drawing pictures, so becoming an illustrator made perfect sense. She currently lives and works in Utah, creating art for children's books, magazines, posters, cards, and anything else people will let her draw on. rebeccasorge.wordpress.com

RACHEL HUNT STEENBLIK researched Heavenly Mother full-time for the *BYU Studies* article, "'A Mother There': A Survey of Historical Teachings about Mother in Heaven." She also authored *Mother's Milk: Poems in Search of Heavenly Mother*, co-edited *Mormon Feminism: Essential Writings*, and writes at *The Exponent* blog. She is a PhD student in philosophy of religion at Claremont Graduate University, and has a BA in philosophy from Brigham Young University and an MS in library and information science from Simmons College.

"I Dreamed I Wrote Five Poems" and "Breathe." *A Mother Here: Art and Poetry Contest* (amotherhere.com), 2014.

"Postpartum," "Tree Rings," and "What Rosemary Taught Me." *Mother's Milk: Poems in Search of Heavenly Mother*. BCC Press, 2017.

ANN GARDNER STONE graduated with honors from Arizona State University with a BA in English and History and an MA in English Language and Education. Ann taught creative writing, literature, and business communication courses at community and junior colleges in Washington, D.C. and Chicago, in addition to developing and presenting training seminars on a wide range of subjects for numerous clients, including the US office of Personnel Management, and the Department of the Navy. She was the Senior Editor and Poetry Editor of *Exponent II*. She co-edited and published a book on pioneer women—*Sister Saints*—and participated in the Ragdale

Foundation poetry workshops. She received first place prizes for her poetry from the *Midwest Poetry Review* and the *Willow Review*. Ann is survived by her two loving sons and two grandchildren.

> "Mother." *Exponent II*, vol. 12, no. 3, 1986, p. 11.

PAUL SWENSON was a Utah journalist whose writing morphed into poetry in the 1990s under the lingering influence of his sister, May Swenson, one of the most anthologized American poets of the 20th Century. His poetry collection, *Iced at the Ward, Burned at the Stake*, was published in 2003 by Signature Books.

> "strange gods." *Sunstone*, no. 107, 1997, p. 44.
> Reprinted in *Iced at the Ward, Burned at the Stake.* Signature Books, 2003.

> "God Plans Her Day" and "Motherless Child." *Iced at the Ward, Burned at the Stake*. Signature Books, 2003.

JAVEN TANNER's poems have appeared in *Midwest Quarterly*, *Roanoke Review*, *Southwestern American Literature*, *Sunstone*, and several other journals and magazines. His collection, *The God Mask*, was recently published. He is the Artistic Director of The Sting & Honey Company and the Dean of Arts at The Waterford School.

> "First Vision." *A Mother Here: Art and Poetry Contest* (amotherhere.com), 2014.

TARA TIMPSON lives in the Southern Utah desert with her husband and five fur kids: four horses and one dog. She works as a veterinarian at an animal sanctuary and enjoys reading, writing, playing bluegrass music, ultra-running, biking, hiking, and playing with her horses.

"Missing Her" and "Small Gifts." *A Mother Here: Art and Poetry Contest* (amotherhere.com), 2014.

NOLA WALLACE was an opera singer, a sculptor, a writer, and a poet. She started her operatic career early—at age 11—taking the bus into Pocatello for voice lessons. She soloed with BYU and later USC and performed at the Hollywood Bowl and Grauman's Chinese Theater. Nola held many church callings over the years, including Relief Society President, cub scout den leader, and cultural refinement instructor. At age 40, she returned to college earning her MA in English Literature.

"A Psalm." *Sunstone*, no. 72, 1989, p. 5. Reprinted in *Mormon Women's Forum Quarterly*, vol. 1, no. 4, 1990, p. 5.

JENNY WEBB is a freelance editor and production manager for academic journals who works in the fields of comparative literature and Mormon studies. Her creative writing has appeared in *Dialogue*, *Wilderness Interface Zone*, and *Times and Seasons*. Jenny lives in Woodinville, Washington, with her husband and two children.

HOLLY WELKER is the editor of *Baring Witness: 36 Mormon Women Talk Candidly about Love, Sex, and Marriage* (University of Illinois Press, 2016). Her poetry and prose have appeared in publications ranging from *Best American Essays* to *Bitch* to *Poetry International* to *The New York Times*.

"God's Muse." *Hayden's Ferry Review*, vol. 19, Fall/Winter 1996.

TERRESA WELLBORN has been published in *BYU Studies Quarterly*, *Fire in the Pasture*, *Monsters & Mormons*, *Dialogue*, and other anthologies and journals. She is a writer, librarian, and poetry editor for *Segullah*. She has a BA degree from Brigham Young University and a MLIS degree from San Jose State University.

TRISH KC BUEL WHEELDON studied creative writing at Brigham Young University–Idaho and ashtanga yoga at 3B Yoga. She doesn't make money from doing either. Most of her time is spent making up metaphors for her life philosophy while pretending to clean, walking in and out of the kitchen deciding what to eat, and trying to get a laugh out of her husband and three children. Connect with her at facebook.com/kcpoet.

RONALD WILCOX was born in Holladay, Utah, in 1934. Educated at BYU, he later received an MA from Baylor, where he studied experimental drama with theatrical innovator Paul Baker. He played the lead role in Thomas Wolfe's *Of Time and* *the River.* This ground-breaking, mixed-media rendition of the novel became the premiere production of the Frank Lloyd Wright-designed Dallas Theater Center (1960). As a Resident Artist in the Professional Repertory Company for 23 years, Ron appeared in over 60 plays. Four of his own plays were produced in Dallas, San Antonio, New York City, Hollywood, and Los Angeles. He designed and directed the premiere of his multi-media poetic drama, *The Tragedy of Thomas Andros* (1964). He has published a novel, *The Rig*. He has contributed to *Dialogue: A Journal of Mormon Thought* since 1967. Two recent volumes of poetry (yet to be published) are entitled *Multiplicity* and *Doggonit Sonnets*, (a collection of 368 new sonnets). Excerpted here are the first four stanzas from "Quantum Gospel," an epic poem of 30 self-contained units. At 83 years of age, Ron continues to write lyric poetry, concentrating on a sonnet form.

Excerpt from "Quantum Gospel: A Mormon Testimony." *Dialogue: A Journal of Mormon Thought*, vol. 40, no. 2, 2007, pp. 168–69.

ADDITIONAL RESOURCES

This limited bibliography, ordered by date, has been included to provide a starting point for further study of the Mormon concept of Heavenly Mother. Many of the resources we've listed address other relevant materials, which readers can pursue for additional understanding.

Linda Wilcox. "The Mormon Concept of a Mother in Heaven." *Sunstone*, no. 5, 1980, pp. 78–87.

Paul and Margaret Toscano. *Strangers in Paradox: Explorations in Mormon Theology*. Signature Books, 1990.

Maxine Hanks. "Toward a Mormon Feminist Theology." Salt Lake Sunstone Symposium, 9 August 1991.

Elaine Anderson Cannon. "Mother in Heaven." *Encyclopedia of Mormonism*. 1992.

Maxine Hanks, editor. *Women and Authority: Re-emerging Mormon Feminism*. Signature Books, 1992.

Janice Allred. "Toward a Mormon Theology of God the Mother." *Dialogue: A Journal of Mormon Thought*, vol. 27, no. 2, Summer 1994, pp. 15–39.

Janice Allred. *God the Mother and Other Theological Essays.* Signature Books, 1997.

Daniel C. Peterson. "Nephi and His Asherah: A Note on 1 Nephi 11:8–23." *Mormons, Scripture, and the Ancient World: Studies in Honor of John L. Sorenson*, edited by Davis Bitton. FARMS, 1998, pp. 191–243.

Maxine Hanks. "Moonstone: Explorations in Feminine Theology." *Sunstone*, no. 133, 2004, pp. 40-41.

Maxine Hanks. "Moonstone: The Hidden Divine Feminine." *Sunstone*, no. 136, 2005, pp. 58-59.

Kevin L. Barney. "How to Worship Our Mother in Heaven (Without Getting Excommunicated)." *Dialogue: A Journal of Mormon Thought*, vol. 41, no. 4, 2008, pp. 121–46.

David Paulsen and Martin Pulido. "'A Mother There': A Survey of Historical Teachings about Mother in Heaven." *BYU Studies Quarterly*, vol. 50, no. 1, 2011, pp. 71–97.

Dan Wotherspoon, Martin Pulido, Tresa Edmunds, and Joanna Brooks. "Heavenly Mother in Today's Mormonism." *Mormon Matters Podcast*, 17 May 2011.

V.H. Casler. "Review of Paulsen and Pulido's 'A Mother There,' *BYU Studies* 2011." *SquareTwo*, vol. 4, no. 1, Spring 2011.

Janice Allred. "The One Who Never Left Us." *Sunstone*, no. 166, 2012, pp. 62–69.

Rachel Hunt Steenblik. "What I First Learned About Heavenly Mother." *Exponent II Blog*, 25 September 2013.

Edward Jones III. "The Mystical Body of God the Mother." *Sunstone*, no. 173, 2013.

"Becoming Like God." *LDS.org*, February 2014, lds.org/topics/becoming-like-god.

A Mother Here: Art and Poetry Contest. Martin Pulido and Caroline Kline, 2014, amotherhere.com.

Margaret Merrill Toscano. "Heavenly Mother's Day: My Search for the Mother." *Exponent II Blog*, 8 May 2015.

Maxine Hanks. "Heavenly Mother's Day: Dreaming of the Divine Feminine." *Exponent II Blog*, 10 June 2015.

Val Larsen. "Hidden in Plain View: Mother in Heaven in Scripture." *SquareTwo*, vol. 8, no. 2, Summer 2015.

"Mother in Heaven." *LDS.org*, October 2015, lds.org/topics/mother-in-heaven.

Joanna Brooks, Rachel Hunt Steenblik, and Hannah Wheelwright, editors. *Mormon Feminism: Essential Writings.* Oxford University Press, 2016.

Caitlin Connolly, Bethany Brady Spalding, and McArthur Krishna. *Our Heavenly Family, Our Earthly Families.* Deseret Book, 2016.

Taylor Petrey. "Rethinking Mormonism's Heavenly Mother." *Harvard Theological Review*, vol. 109, no. 3, 2016, pp. 315–41.

Rachel Hunt Steenblik. *Mother's Milk: Poems in Search of Heavenly Mother.* Illustrated by Ashley Mae Hoiland. BCC Press, 2017.

Russell Stevenson, Rachel Steenblik, and Caitlin Connolly. "A Heavenly Mother—Rachel Steenblik and Caitlin Connolly." *LDS Perspectives Podcast*, 10 May 2017.

Gina Colvin and Rachel Hunt Steenblik. "206: Mother's Milk: Poems in Search of Heavenly Mother: Rachel Hunt Steenblik." *A Thoughtful Faith Podcast*, 14 August 2017.

April Young Bennett, Rachel Hunt Steenblik, and Ashley Mae Hoiland. "The Mormon Concept of Heavenly Mother with Rachel Hunt Steenblik and Ashley Mae Hoiland." *The Religious Feminism Podcast*, 20 August 2017.